What people are saying about

Lupa - She-Wolf of Rome and Mother of Destiny

Through her heartfelt, playful prose Rachel unlocks deep echoes of primal remembering rarely felt. This is divine feminine soul retrieval at its best! I am so proud of her!

Katie Holland, Creator of Awakened Belly Dance

Rachel brings the story of Romulus and Remus into divine perspective, focusing her attention instead on Lupa, the She-Wolf that they suckle from. This book has opened my eyes to 'what came before' the beginning of Rome and strikes a chord with my understanding of the inherent 'Mother Goddess' that roamed BEFORE the patriarchy and in a time when both woman and men had equal status. A great read with insightful guidance for those wishing to deepen their relationship with Lupa.

Melonie Syrett, The Drum Woman

Through Rachel's words, The Sacred She-Wolf drew me into Her energy, and I could feel Her around me as I read more and more about Her origins, stories and traditions, coming out of the other side of the book with a newfound understanding and a love of the fierce energy that is Lupa! It is of paramount importance that we stand together to bring these ancient stories of the Divine Feminine back into the world. Thank you for your offering, Rachel, a vital read.

Kat Shaw, Artist

Pagan Portals
Lupa

She-Wolf of Rome and Mother of Destiny

Pagan Portals

Lupa

She-Wolf of Rome and Mother of Destiny

Rachel S Roberts

MOON
BOOKS

Winchester, UK
Washington, USA

JOHN HUNT PUBLISHING

First published by Moon Books, 2023
Moon Books is an imprint of John Hunt Publishing Ltd., No. 3 East Street, Alresford
Hampshire SO24 9EE, UK
office@jhpbooks.net
www.johnhuntpublishing.com
www.moon-books.net

For distributor details and how to order please visit the 'Ordering' section on our website.

Text copyright: Rachel S Roberts 2022

ISBN: 978 1 80341 350 1
978 1 80341 351 8 (ebook)
Library of Congress Control Number: 2022944262

A CIP catalogue record for this book is available from the British Library.

Design: Lapiz Digital Services

UK: Printed and bound by CPI Group (UK) Ltd, Croydon, CR0 4YY
Printed in North America by CPI GPS partners

We operate a distinctive and ethical publishing philosophy in
all areas of our business, from our global network of authors to
production and worldwide distribution.

Contents

To Mum, David, Trish and Matt, with much gratitude for all of your support and encouragement, because every she-wolf needs her loving pack to feed her, run with her and to listen to the endless howling of random historical facts instead of normal conversation! Thank you!

Raging beast and raging flood
Alike have spared the prey;
And today the dead are living;
The lost are found today.

The troubled river knew them,
And smothered his yellow foam,
And gently rocked the cradle
That bore the fate of Rome.
The ravening she-wolf knew them,
And licked them o'er and o'er,
And gave them of her own fierce milk,
Rich with raw flesh and gore.
T.B, Macaulay 19th Century

Timeline of Ancient Rome
(and significant events mentioned in this book)

c.1100 – 900 BCE	Villanovan Culture in Central Italy
c.900 – 750 BCE	Beginning of the Etruscan Civilisation in Central Italy
c.800 BCE	Etruscan archaeological evidence found of first village settlement on the Palatine Hill
753 BCE	Mythical founding date of Rome by Romulus on Palatine Hill
650 – 510 BCE	Etruscan Kings - building of Rome from town to city
c.500 BCE	Statue of the Bronze Capitoline she-wolf created
509 BCE	Rome becomes a Republic, run by elected Senators
396 BCE	Roman expansion begins with the capture of the city of Veii from the Etruscans. Signals the end of independent Etruscan culture
65 BCE	Lightning bolt hits she-wolf statue and is documented by Cicero
45 BCE	End of the Republic. Julius Caesar becomes the first dictator
27 BCE	Roman Empire begins - Augustus Caesar becomes first Roman Emperor
306 CE	Emperor Constantine converts to Christianity. Rome becomes a Christian Empire in 380 CE
476 CE	The last Western Roman Emperor, Romulus Augustus, is deposed by the mercenary, Odoacer, who becomes the first king of Italy. Signals fall of ancient Rome and start of the Early Middle Ages

European timeline
All dates are approximate.

700,000 – 2500 BCE	Stone Age
2500 – 700 BCE	Bronze Age
700 BCE – 400 CE	Iron Age
400 CE onwards	Early Middle Ages

Central Italy

c.1100 – c.900 BCE	Villanovan Culture
c.900 – c.200 BCE	Etruscan Civilisation (146 BCE Subjection to Rome)
509 BCE – 476 CE	Roman Civilisation

Preface

She-Wolves and Queenship

Many years ago, for my BA Honours Degree in History and Religious Studies I was again and again drawn to Queenship. As a result, I became a truly passionate and devoted advocate for the medieval queens of England and took it quite to heart when they were maligned.

What intrigued me the most was the term she-wolf that the queens were frequently labelled with, used really as the worst sort of bad-naming and intended as the most offensive criticism possible. My dissertation went on to explore the ideals and expectations of queenship in comparison to the reality and the actual experiences of the queens themselves.

During my research, whenever the term she-wolf came up it almost became an alarm bell for me. I began to learn that when it did arise, the Queen was doing or saying something I should take notice of, and was almost always something I was cheering her on for. What I saw in these she-wolves were woman striving for independence, for recognition, for a sliver of respect for herself as a woman, or even just as a person. The label 'she-wolf' came up when the queens had been seeking to take ownership of their bodies and their lives.

When a woman was described as a she-wolf in these medieval times and also earlier in the Roman context of our she-wolf, Lupa, it was a term to highlight a woman as wild and untamed as a wolf, when often she was just pushing and pulling at her patriarchal bonds.

Queens and poor women alike were labelled as she-wolves when they attempted independence from men and so she-wolf became a derogatory term insinuating rebelliousness and a divergence from the norm that was decided by someone other than herself.

In some cases, as with the Lupa of the Lupanar in Pompeii, whom I will share more about in this book, the term she-wolf was also a term used for prostitutes, considered the woman who was lowest of the low and a predator leading man astray.

Since my dissertation I have always been curious about any woman labelled as a she-wolf and now personally wear that title as a badge of honour. I hear the name she-wolf as a call from deep within, I feel it as the wolf hears her call from the far-off pack. I now know that in this being brought to my notice I was one of the she-wolf's pups being called back to sit at the feet of the Wolf Mother to relearn about the value and sacredness of the parts of me, like with the Queens, that are deemed too much, too uncontrolled, too loud, too frightening. She is a wild animal. She is untamed, she is wild and fierce, powerful and dangerous to those that seek to confine or control her.

You will see a woman become the she-wolf when she is making a stand for her freedom and integrity and seeking alignment with her truth amidst the bounds of societal pressure, judgement and opinion.

All of this is the motivating fire behind this book, the call I heard most strongly from Lupa herself, to share the sacredness within her story and of her women, so that they may be seen, heard, witnessed and honoured. Perhaps this is even part of a reclaiming of the term she-wolf.

There is truly a wolf within us all that longs to howl loud and clear our unique frequency, desires and truth. And there is a longing even deeper, I think, to be truly heard and to hear a howl back that says 'I hear you; I see you, and I'm coming along for the ride'. From behind a Roman doorway, you are now hearing a womb deep call of the wild, from your Wolf Mother, saying I am here, are you ready?

So, I acknowledge your dear presence here, thank you for reading this book. Myself and Lupa are truly honoured that you are listening and choosing to run along-side us.

Introduction

In many cultures, myths and legends there are wolves depicted, from cave paintings, to traditional fables and modern-day film and television. Often their role in these depictions is to represent the themes of power, strength, underworld travel and entry, death, instinct and vision in the darkness. Wolves capture the imagination and, I believe, stir something deep within us that remembers that first encounter of wolf and man on the hunt, which still pulses in our blood and lives on in our companionship with dogs.

The story of Lupa, which lies at the centre of this book, is of the time of the ancient Romans. Rooted in Roman mythology, Lupa is the primary depiction of a she-wolf that has been left to us from classical antiquity. Certainly, she is the only named wolf, who plays a role of central and undisputed importance. There are sometimes Gods and Goddess's, such as Mars and Diana, that are occasionally depicted with a wolf companion or the ability to command and communicate with the wolves, or wild beasts in general. It was, after all, common for the characteristics of the deities of our ancient worlds to be symbolised by an animal totem. In Rome, for example, Jupiter is often shown with or as his eagle and Juno with her peacock or geese.

What is different about Lupa is not just that she can be a wolf, but that she is a she-wolf. She is not ethereal, disconnected from us or living above and beyond the human realm. She is not an otherwise distant being that only transforms into an animal when she wishes to influence someone or something. She is the full embodiment of raw, wild feminine primal power, living and breathing in the strong and fierce body of a wolf. As the she-wolf, she is the Goddess that is nature and the Goddess that takes a very present and active supporting role in our lives.

As wolf she is that which has the ability and courage to destroy and create and she is that which knows, sees and embraces what lies in the dark *and* the light and so she is life and death simultaneously.

The she-wolf is of a time when the Goddess who, like the bird and snake goddesses of the Neolithic peoples, was the embodiment and manifestation of Nature. She is the inherent life force within us, the wild and untamed beauty of the natural world.

She is the part of that which lies within all of us, no matter our physical gender, or age or background. Within us all lies this primal mother, this archetype or aspect of ourself that calls to be remembered and utilised.

Through her you will remember and witness in your own life the sacred relationship of knowledge and wisdom. Wisdom is knowledge when it is experienced and embodied; our heads may be full but we must return it home to our body, as our earth and foundation, and there assimilate, create, transform and transmute. In her myths, the twin boys Romulus and Remus must return to her before they can follow their paths of kingship. They must meet the she-wolf, be suckled by her, receive her wisdom and enter the cave as initiation. And so, the she-wolf will take all into her cave, so that knowledge can became wisdom, for what use is knowledge if not channelled into service, purpose, compassion and loving action?

In this book I first of all share the her-story of Lupa, the she-wolf, Mother of the Eternal City. We will begin with an exploration of Her-story, as it was known and experienced by the ancient Romans and we will explore what they left to us through primary sources of art, archaeology and written word. Then I will also share the wisdom and messages that have come through directly from her to me during communion, and from experiencing and walking her path and mythos. We hope this combination will uniquely manifest in remembrance and enlightenment for you and that you will come to know her as both historical, mythical figure and as aspect of the Divine Feminine.

We only have one story of Lupa, one instance left to us through mythology but what an insightful and a powerful story it is! You will find sandwiched between the history and spiritual connection chapters, a re-telling of her story, in Lupa's own voice channelled through me, her words, her essence and what she wants to be heard at this time. You may want to read this book in the order I have offered, or you may want to read the story first, feel into what is right for you.

And so, in this sharing She steps forth now on mighty paws to reclaim her seat and stage. She has been waiting a long time to work with us in this way. You may have already had encounters, glimpses of something stirring within the dark of her cave, but if you are holding and reading this book, it is time for you to work more deeply with her. She has so much to offer beyond the limitations of recorded history and truly her unique offering to humankind is that of facilitator and midwife in remembering and enabling your unique blueprint. She will support and guide you in living a life of embodied destiny. She will remind you of your pure potentiality and together you will journey to discover and create a life courageously lived on-purpose.

When sharing her mythology often historians' comment on the astonishing coincidence of Lupa finding the twins at the river's edge. Even more so that it was pure luck that a child laden basket arrived nowhere else but at the feet of a politically sympathetic wolf (and also pretty handy the babies were too cute to have made a great breakfast for a wild and untamed predator).

But as we know from our own life's journeys, there is no coincidence, and believing it was such, so there lies a misunderstanding of Her way and truth. We may seem to stumble upon experiences, people and places in life but there is always a thread, a path of preparation to those destined spots. In truth, she was there waiting at the river side at the time that was always meant to be.

She was there, ready, because there is a destiny, a divine purpose for us all, that is fulfilled when we are ready to trust and receive. She knew and so will you know.

She was there all along, waiting at the riverside of the Tiber and now she is there waiting for you also.

So come let us journey with our Wolf Mother.

Chapter 1

Lupa in Ancient Roman History

Setting the Scene

Legends about deities form a large part of the background to religion. The stories and myths provide the substance, source and inspiration for many rituals, superstitions and devotional acts and feelings alike. This mythos is found depicted everywhere from homes, to clothes, to tombs, to tools, to food and temples, displaying the importance and perhaps also emotional impact of religious story to the practitioner.

Lupa, is the she-wolf that features in the mythos of Romulus and Remus and the foundation story of Rome. In recognition of her centrality to ancient Roman life, she is called by the Roman politician and writer, Cicero, *"The Nurse of Roman dominion."*[1] We will see throughout this book that the story of Lupa is an exemplary example of the true impact that one story can indeed have on a culture and belief system.

Throughout its history Rome rose from a small town, to an expanding republic, then finally manifested as an empire that dominated the known world. The empire stretched from Jordan to Scotland and right at the centre stands a solitary she-wolf whose choice and loving action enabled it all to manifest. At the root of the power of Rome lies the nurturing, protective, primal and fierce energy of the Feminine.

She began by suckling and then keeping safe two babes within her cave dwelling and then, throughout the rise of Rome, she became an evocative symbol of the city and power of the Roman state. She was the protector of the Eternal City and sits in central importance at the foundations and deepest origins of a city that was home to one of the most influential empires in history, known for its military and political might.

For the empire, the she-wolf was a guarantee of prosperity, divine favour and survival. For as long as the Roman nation was protected by the she-wolf, it would thrive.

However, the wolf also would have been well known to the farmer and every day man as a predator. By the time of the Roman Empire, the wolf would have been pushed to the outskirts of society, perhaps more often heard than seen and whose identity would be mixed up with a lot of fear and dread.

Despite this, in the mythos of Lupa that I will share in this chapter, the legendary she-wolf saves the founding twins of the city of Rome. We see her in this story not as a deadly predator, but as a divine instigator, not a wolf side-lined to the bad guy in a cautionary story, but as the care-taking and life-giving facilitation of Mother Nature. Often in ancient sources it is her nurturing and life-saving involvement in the lives of two child humans that elevates her from mere wolf to divine. Yet we will explore in this book how Lupa is also an ambassador and manifestation of the divine essence of she-wolf. It is not just the act of rescue that makes her divine, but rather it is *because* she is a Goddess in and of herself that she chooses to offer her unique facilitation for the twins and so acts as the divine catalyst, steering them on their path of destiny.

Sometimes this divine essence has been lost in the patriarchal intent of the retelling of her story. We will explore how later Roman historians documented her story, often briefly, with her performing merely a function or role in service of a male god, or male humans.

Lupa literally means she-wolf in Latin, with Lupus as the masculine equivalent. She is all that is encompassed in that one, seemingly small word; power, courage, leader, fierce, protective. Yet later the word Lupa also becomes a term used by the Romans for low-level prostitutes and women, not an exemplar of the ideal Roman Matron (much as these days we would use the derogatory term bitch in an attempt to offend a woman we wish to judge and label as wrong). We will explore more of these women and share their story later on at the end of this chapter. Both Lupa and these women named after her both share a need to be recognised, remembered and honoured. But let us first begin with a brief introduction to the story itself.

The foundation story in which Lupa features it set at the beginning of the 700's BCE in central Italy. There are a few variations in the story as it is told later in history but here are some of the main and most commonly repeated features.

The King of Alba Longa, Amulius, usurps the throne of his brother Numitor. Through his jealousy and fear Amulius orders the death of his two twin -grandnephews, Romulus and Remus. They are ordered to be drowned in the river Tiber. However, the orders are defied and the babies are instead put onto the river in a basket. The river is swollen with winter rain and the basket is carried to the shore and is caught up in the roots of a fig tree. The basket containing the babies is found by the she-wolf who takes them into her care and suckles them as they cry in hunger. After some time, a gang of men, possibly soldiers from Amulius, come to kill the babes, but the she-wolf fiercely protects them as her own, defending them and scaring off the would-be attackers. She then takes them to her cave and there she nursed and cared for them until they later left the cave and were raised by the farmer-deity Faustulus.

However, one day Romulus returns to the hill in honour of that connection and care-taking from the Mother Goddess in Wolf form. Fast forward a few years and a few more stories and Romulus becomes the founder and first king of the city of Rome. In remembrance of his time within the cave, Romulus chooses the Hill, known to us now as Palatine, as the location for his new kingdom, founding the first major settlement in this location. And so, this story is the beginning of Rome, and of the first known and recorded co-creationship between Lupa and man.

Interestingly, however, the story does not stand alone with its involvement of a she-wolf protector. In other ancient Italian cities and tribes there are similar stories to that of Lupa and Rome. The foundation myth of Lavinium (a port city of Latium, four miles south of Rome) also involves the hero of the tale being rescued and fed by a she-wolf. Also, ancient sources tell of Sabine families in central Italy being guided by a she-wolf to find safety and new land. It could be argued that these she-wolves were the divine guides that knew the paths of their land, both practically and energetically and this is why the Sabine wolf and Lupa both determined the locations for the new kingdoms, bringing their people to these places. So, perhaps we should begin with the questions why a wolf?

In relation to our story of Lupa, being nursed and reared by a wolf in the wild was believed to have encouraged Roman virtus in the two children; that is courage, toughness, valour and prudence, all needed by a man if he were to become a leader and king. Their time with her as teacher and guide made them men, as it was through her milk that her characteristics and strengths were passed on.

In this myth she also acts as rescuer, nurturer and fierce protector. All of these are the potent medicine of the wolf. The she-wolf as the leader of her pack is both maternal, discerning and wise. She is also a personification of the innate wisdom and knowing of nature, and of the mother. Her instinct guides her and she follows it with courage. The most commonly used descriptive word used for Lupa in ancient sources is 'ferocity' and nowhere is this displayed more than in the courageous protection of her young and pack. When witnessing wolf packs and alpha she-wolf's even now these innate skill in strategy, teamwork, tenacity and leadership are profoundly apparent. Wolves unite to protect every member of their pack, whether young or old, healthy or wounded.

Lupa is the one specifically destined for these children. For their lives and legacy, it is her lineage, skills and knowledge that is called upon. She is more than just rescuer; she is the divine and cosmic milk nurse that is the facilitator of destiny. Through her actions she acts as an example and teacher. With courage and devotion, she approaches her role of keeper and protector of divine purpose. And so, in fulfilling her own destiny she shows us how to embody our own.

Her symbolic archetype for us, then, is a lesson and guide to us of the potential power and value of maternal care. She shows us how we can embody the primal mother archetype in our self-care; self-sourcing our fulfilment and learning to trust our instinct. She teaches us how to fiercely protect the sacred and holy within us that may feel vulnerable or small, as well as reminding us to offer this protection also to those threatened and in need in the world around us. She also guides us to take responsibility and action in pursuing and living our unique path and purpose, again for ourselves as well as humanity.

We will explore more deeply the story's meaning and messages for us in Chapter 3. Let us first dive a little deeper now into the foundations and contextual history of this myth so that we can get a glimpse into what it meant for the ancient Romans.

The foundation story of Rome sits before the time that the city was even established. To find the first threads of our story therefore we must look further back. We will explore now how Lupa's mythos and essence is actually woven in earlier Etruscan history, beliefs and culture. So, it is with Etruria where we begin.

Part 1: Etruscan Wolf Goddess

At the time of the foundation myth of Rome the most powerful and richest peoples of central Italy were the Etruscans. When we first hear of Lupa as the she-wolf and patroness of a small, farming settlement called Rome, the Roman Empire was a long way in the future. In fact, her central importance in the foundation story highlights that she was already in the minds and hearts of pre-Roman peoples. She is the sole representation of the divine and divine presence in the earliest foundation mythos and so can quite rightly be given the title Divine Mother of Rome. We can also see in art and archaeological evidence that the Etruscans and Villanovans peoples of the foundation time were acquainted with wolves, whether through personally or though story, religion and art and had their own ideas and perspective on the wolf.

The time within which Lupa's mythos originates, Etruscan culture and influence was at its peak and they were the most prominent peoples in central Italy. It was a civilisation rooted in the earliest indigenous cultures of Italy, in the area between the rivers Aron and the Tiber. The Etruscans themselves are believed to be the descendants of the earlier Villanovans (see timeline).[2]

The Etruscan peoples lived in huts, which, like their temples, were circular in shape, and usually built of wood or mud and decorated with terracotta reliefs and statues. Stone was kept for tombs and fortifications. Many tombs, often in the shape of huts or houses[3] were built or carved into rock faces like caves and there is evidence of rituals or dedications actually made in caves also. A vault was created inside the mountain or hillside, returning the dead like seeds to soil. We can perhaps speculate here the symbology in the minds of the Etruscans of the cave within the hillside as the beginning of the journey of death and as the doorway then onto the next stage. We see this cave symbology, with the cave as a transitionary place, playing an important part in Lupa's story.

The Etruscans are also credited with innovation of adopting the arch into art and sculpture, which was then subsequently adapted into Roman architecture and it was also a culture that was optimized by its celebrated and prolific bronze work.

The Etruscan cities reached the height of their splendour and power between the seventh and fifth centuries BCE. Rather than a united-state, Etruscan culture was a confederation of 12 city states that were individually governed by a ruler known as the Lucumo, and for reasons of defence, built on high ground, which we can imagine led to the choice of the hills of Rome. However, the location of Rome was also an ideal spot for more reasons than one. Commerce was the source of the prosperity of the Etruscans and the area where they built their new settlement was not only a hill but right next to the Tiber, the most significant river in central Italy. The Etruscan's were known for their maritime supremacy in the Western Mediterranean and it was this supremacy as well as trade that led to the richness of the culture and economy.

It seems that the first people to settle in the location of Rome were Etruscans expanding (or fleeing) to new areas. Both close links and Etruscan influence remained strong long after their migration to the new settlement and we know of named Etruscan kings ruling Rome from c.650 to c.510 BCE.

In many ways these first peoples were quite different to the later Romans. For example, Etruscan women were regarded as equal members of society with their male counterparts. James Wellard even goes so far as to say that *"their liberated condition, in fact was unique in the ancient world"* [4] and the Etruscan status of women was looked on with scorn by the Greeks and then later Romans who described the Etruscan people as prostitutes (Lupas) so free were they in comparison with the ideal of the Roman Matron.

In their tombs paintings we see a sensual people, living life to the full. There are depictions of laughter and the joys of friendship, with enough affectionate closeness between spouses to have really upset Roman sensibilities. There are even scenes of Etruscans playing together in the sea! Their tombs show the clear ideal of married love and affection, that was openly expressed and displayed in everyday life, along with a respectful and celebratory role for women. Many tombs also included inscriptions referencing mother and father, indicating the importance of the mother's side of the family and the female lineage, as well as the father's. Much to my personal joy there is also depiction after depiction of dancing! Dances of family, dances of celebration, ritual and ecstasy, as well as seemingly just for the sheer joy of it! Dancing was frequently enjoyed outdoors in and with nature. Often accompanying these dancers is a person playing the flute, which gives us an insightful insight into the sounds of Etruria and some argue an early connection to the god, Pan.

This was a culture within which the feminine was celebrated as an important and contributory force in itself, not merely a functional role. It is easy to see Lupa as part of this, acting independently and with confidence, with an undeniable importance and authority in the mythos.

Also interesting for our journey with Lupa is that the shrine for the 'national' or supreme god, Voltumna (also known as Veltha) was not the temples of the later Roman Empire but a 'sacred grove' of earth and trees called Fanum Voltumnae. Both his sacred grove and his un-human nature (depicted as non-gendered vegetation) are representative of the early Etruscan divine and belief system. Which we will explore in more detail now.

Religion and the Etruscan Wolf

Being all wolf, and not a shapeshifter, Lupa often reminds me of the Neolithic and Palaeolithic oneness of divine and nature, the she-wolf that prowled the cave paintings and dreams of our oldest ancestors as mother and sister. When we came to later Roman religion, she seems out of place with the later Roman deities who have human form and voice. There is no other deity of the Roman Pantheon that is solely and only in animal form and so she must have been roaming the forests long before the establishment of the Roman belief system.

Etruria made the first and most important contribution to the formation of Roman religion and it is here perhaps that we can see that bridge on which Lupa seems to sit; a bridge between old and new beliefs systems.

The early Etruscan and Villanovan deities were still the old nature gods of the more ancient ancestors, rather than the humanised deities of Greece and later Rome. For the Etruscans the divine was the force and uncontrollable power of Nature and sometimes the divine was honoured as local earth or elemental Spirits. On occasion we do see a lingering of earlier belief systems within the Roman pantheon. For examples of the Etruscan legacy, we can look to the Roman Vesta as The Fire/Flame, Lupa as The Wolf and the River Tiber, as father Tiber, an elemental guardian of the water. The local elemental spirits often had no form but their natural state of tree, animal or wind but were later individualised by the Romans and became a particular singular divinity with human form and characteristics. We see a trend that happens with both Greek and then Roman deities from animism (*the belief in a divinity or spiritual essence within all creatures, places and objects*) to more often anthropomorphism (*a god, animal or object being given human characteristics, behaviour or form*). We see this threshold of change of the gods from Nature's image to Man's image throughout the Bronze age through into the Iron age.

Perhaps we could then speculate that, the she-wolf that becomes Lupa to the Romans, a named and singular figure, may have her origin as part of a wild earth or nature essence or even the energy form of the 'The She-Wolf'.

Lupa also roams the land before the human to animal shape-shifting of Greek influence from the 6th century onwards and she does not have any equivalent in Greek Mythology, nor was she amalgamated in the way that Jupiter-Zeus and Juno-Hera were. Mostly the Romans also amalgamated the Etruscan deities, such as Aphrodite (Greek) was associated with both the Etruscan Turo, 'The Lady' and the Etruscan Venus (a vegetation deity) in reaction to their similarities. Yet Lupa was not matched to any comparative form in Greek Mythology, she was not 'associated' with any other deity in other belief systems, but stood alone, unique.

The Etruscan and earlier gods were also not partnered up into couples like the Greek and later Roman Pantheon. It was only as the power and might of early Rome grew and was influenced by Greek culture that the gods came to incorporate their own form of politics and human style relationships, personalities, vices and virtues. Lupa, She-Wolf, features in her story more like an Etruscan nature spirit, a stand-alone force of nature under no authority or influence from any other.

For our journey with Lupa we must also note the prominent Villanovan and Etruscan belief that the gods determined the fate, destiny and fortune of every individual. This wasn't a people that could take fate in their own hands like Hercules. If the divine decreed that a man was born a king or a slave, that was his pre-destined fate and there was nothing that he could do about it.

We can see this reflected in Lupa's personal involvement in saving and raising the twins. Her choice cemented the fate not just of two men but of a whole country and empire.

For these peoples all was also interdependent and what affected one part affected the whole, the like a stone creating a ripple when dropped by the water. The ripple is felt by every drop of water in the lake and like this, arguably the whole history of Europe was determined by Lupa's one decision to suckle rather than destroy.

The Etruscans looked for signs from the gods in nature and used divination to discover what was their will. They practiced hepatoscopy (liver divination) and observed the flight of birds. They also noted natural phenomenon such as shooting stars, thunder and lightning. The direction, volume, timing and point of contact of the thunderbolt were a clear message as well as an indication as to which deity was making themselves known. There were believed to be 11 types of thunderbolts, each was an individual voice of the gods. So, by observation you knew exactly who was sending a message and what about.

Lupa's story contains this Etruscan fatalistic belief in destiny and the immutable course of divine will in which the lives of men were pre-ordained. In the foundation story we witness Lupa as a direct intervention of the divine in steering purpose and destiny.

The Wolf and Death

It is interesting to note that the Etruscan word 'Lupu' means 'to die', with the word Lupus referring to "the dead". For the Etruscans the wolf was linked into the symbolism of death, especially through their entering of the cave into an unknown darkness, an entrance the humans believed must allow the wolves to roam freely into the otherworld/underworld. The she-wolf especially is known to make the cave her place of retreat. She would enter the cave and to the outside world her time within contained completely unknown activity. It may have seemed, therefore, that the wolf had free reign and guardianship of the entry ways that led down into the womb of the earth. The cave became a place of threshold and rebirth. This must have been affirmed when the she-wolves would return out of the cave with cubs a few months later.

There was also a 'masculine' wolf that has an association with death in Etruscan religion. The most well-known wolf image of Etruscan history is Charun, the 'monster' with the head of a black wolf, flaming eyes and large fangs and has a large hammer to crush skulls. The word monster is used by historians and archaeologists because he has no definite form, but is a typical Etruscan mix of nature, elements and animal. Historians have defined Charun to be the God of the Etruscan Underworld and so through him, to some extent, the Etruscan image of the wolf is now linked to the underworld. However, we have no way of knowing if he was considered along the same lines as well Hades, Pluto or even Cerberus, the many headed hound who guarded the gates to the Grecian underworld.

Charun does not seem either to have any relation to the she-wolf and is never depicted with a feminine counter-part. He is, though, depicted with his companion Tuchulcha, a mix of vulture, donkey and snake and it was he that was the giver of nightmares.

Archaeological evidence places the manifestation of both of these gods at the same time as Lupa's story. We see them arising in Etruscan tomb and funerary art in the mid-300's BCE at the time when Etruscan culture was itself in its death throes, and the fear of destruction by Rome was deeply ingrained into the minds and hearts of the last Etruscan people. At this time, it seems that the afterlife was viewed as a terrifying place, just as life may have also seemed. So, Lupa may not be associated to Charun but we can takeaway that there was an important relation between the wolf and death.

Charun and Lupa are the only two known wolves in Etruscan myth. In Etruscan art it is the snake and horse that are most frequently depicted, but not the wolf. This may be explained by the fact that the snake and horse would have been frequent players in the lives of these people, unlike the wolf who was not seen or known. The wolves lived on the outskirts, in the forests, the dark places, the caves and where they lived was unknown, out of sight from man. Wolves hunt mostly at night when man is not around and so most people would only hear their hungry howls throughout the dark, lean times of this year. The wolf that once hunted with man was for the majority mostly an unseen, unknown entity by this time in history. It is very probable that the only time they came into contact was as a roaming predator in the peripheral vision or seen retreating into and emerging from their cave or forest sanctuaries.

This wolf association with the dark, the night, the cave and so also death does not then seem a surprise.

We also find wolves in other pre-Roman and ancient Italian wolf cults such as the Hirpi Sorani. In Faliscan culture *hirpus* was the Faliscan word for wolf. Here the wolf was an underworld deity and again we see myths of wolves and the caves in mountains being gateways to the underworld in which wolves entered and exited this world.

Is Lupa, then, perhaps a Goddess of Life and Death, the two intrinsically linked through her retreat to the cave? Is it just a cave that Lupa takes the twins to in her story? Or is it also a symbolic passage and a journey through the shadows and darkness, into the womb of the earth itself?

As a personification of Mother Earth, Lupa's womb-cave is the underworld, the inner world, the great below and the great unknown. In almost all of the records of Lupa's story it is to her cave that Lupa takes the twins either to suckle or protect them. So, it is here, therefore, in the safe but dark sanctuary that they grow and *become*. In the Etruscan telling of this story this aspect cannot have but reminded them of their cave tombs and temples, as well as the wolf entrances to the otherworld.

Etruscan Conclusion

From this background we can conclude that Lupa seems to fit right into the nature-based spirits of the Etruscan culture, that personally determined the fate of humankind. Also, that the inclusion of the cave retreat would have had spiritual and iconic importance in the foundation story. There is something perhaps even in the larger psyche that associates the wolf of the cave, with the nurturing and live giving Divine Mother.

Much of Etruscan history is lost to us, there may be more of the she-wolf yet unknown, there certainly does seem some gaps in trying to determine her specific historical origins. So many artefacts and archaeology of this period has been destroyed and the little we do know of this culture comes mostly from tombs. Therefore, the evidence, in the form of sculpture, paintings, furnishing is funerary in nature and although life is depicted, it is within the context of death. Though the depictions of the she-wolf are sparce we can see the influences on the mythos of Lupa from the Etruscan, and perhaps earlier, belief system.

So, from the cave she remerged to bring the She-Wolf again into a new era and from Etruscan foundations a journey began which would end with her legacy as Rome itself.

Part 2: A Roman Story and Sacred Beginnings

One of the most potent ways in which humans can explore or deepen their identity of self is by expressing it through the artistic portrayal of their deities and religion. Why does a particular animal become the mascot or emblem of a culture or town? Why is a particular story told generation after generation? They all carry a message, a code, a symbol of affirmation of who we are. What we all need is a sense of belonging and deities provide this as the particular focus of our united devotion, dedication and confirmation/validation. For the ancient Romans they were the people of the she-wolf. This patriarchal and masculine driven and controlled empire of Rome was symbolised by the nourishing, protective and courageous energy of the Wolf Mother. The ancient Romans all became Romulus and Remus, under her protection and were strengthened by the milk of her essence.

The origin stories of Lupa, she-wolf and Mother of the Eternal City, is shrouded in some mystery and uncertainty as far as archaeology and written history goes. The foundation myths were known and passed down through oral history and art, to then be written down later from the 1st C. BCE onwards by men firmly born and raised in the Roman Republic, then Empire. However, the story had become so important as part of national identity for the ancient Romans that even Augustus Caesar gained validation through claiming descent from Romulus. The legions of the Roman army also took Lupa as an emblem on military wear to remind them of the ferocity and fearlessness they could embody as one of Rome's wolf sons and fighters.

Let's now explore the importance of Lupa and her story for a growing Rome and the place of her mythos in Ancient Roman identity, symbology and belief. Let us see how when we look a little beyond the forceful characteristics of the fighting power and dominating authority of the Roman Empire we find here, as with all things, that at the foundation lies the Mother, She who gives and grows life.

Goddess of Threshold and Initiation

The foundation story of Lupa and the Twins lies within the early years of the 700s BCE.

753 BCE is given as the date for the legendary founding of the city of Rome by Romulus. It was in 753 BCE[5] that, according to myth, Romulus became sole King of Rome, reigning until approximately 717.BC. The earliest settlements of Rome were centred around enclosed areas of certain hills, keeping the occupation above the marshlands that were liable to flooding and mosquitos.

At the time of Lupa's story the area was well-wooded. These thick, deep forests were still prevalent even in the southern areas of Etruria at the end of the 4th century. The forests were even formidable enough to inspire fear in the hearts of Roman soldiers! In 311BCE there was a battle between Roman and Etruscan city states. After defeat, the Etruscans fled into the forest that covered the Ciminian range and the Roman army was too scared to follow until given some quite persuasive encouragement from their general! These forests of elm, beech, oak, pine, maple and willow were the roaming grounds of the wolves. Most wolves were likely still never to have been seen, only heard, by most people but were known to roam these dark and wild places.

Romulus's Rome has humble origins as a small settlement of farmers. Archaeologists have found evidence of the round huts which were the homes of the very first peoples on Palatine Hill and there are many contemporary references to a 'Hut of Romulus' that continued to be preserved and rebuilt well into the time of Emperor Augustus. Also, the hill has at its south-west foot a cave, this cave is where the threads of Rome began and is called the Lupercal, home of Lupa.

The first peoples of this region and earliest settlement of Rome were perhaps Latins from over-populated Alba Longa (south of present-day Rome) or Etruscans from Veii (nine miles north of present-day Rome). Most historians believe that these people were Etruscan who were either outcasts or migrants and it seems that the archaeological evidence found for the first settlement on Palatine Hill is Etruscan in nature.

The first Romans then, as are wolves, were those living on the outskirts of society but also pioneers. They were truly like the roaming pack in spring; wolves venturing and travelling to lands as yet unknown to begin anew.

Lupa's story, however, lies at a pivotal time not just for the foundation story of Rome and Roman history but also in the transitionary period of European history at the end of the bronze age and the beginning of the iron age. This time was one when lives were changing both on the large and small scale.

As a present guide and guardian at this transitional time, Lupa is a threshold Goddess in more ways than one, she is a mid-wife that ushers in a new era. In this aspect she is also the Goddess that bestows the divine right of kingship upon Romulus through her appearance and facilitation at this pivotal moment.

The mythos is typical of the close interrelationships between Divine and Man in the Ancient World and also of the Goddess as Initiator. The story is one of the rites and right of kingship being bestowed upon man by the Goddess, which is itself a reoccurring theme in bronze age religions and cultures. In the arriving of a basket containing the sons of destiny upon the riverbank we are reminded of a story retold again and again. We see this pivotal part of the story repeated in other similar myths such as the well-known stories of Moses in Egypt and Taliesin in Wales and lesser-known stories such as the ancient Sumerian King Sargon. Sargon was born to a temple priestess and unknown father and was cast into the river in a basket of rushes. He is later rescued by a divine being who in saving the child displays their favour and offers a blessing of greatness. King Sargon is noted to be favoured by the Goddess Inanna, who was involved in saving him and he later goes onto to become a great king and founds a city in her honour. The story is exceptionally similar to that of Lupa and the foundation of Rome. Similar myths also surround Attis, consort-son of Cybele, who as a baby was found washed up in the reeds of the river Gallus.

These stories offer a remembrance or affirmation of the initiation rites of kingship guided and facilitated by Nature and the Divine Feminine. The king is not just king through hereditary father to son descent as occurs later in history but through this direct involvement and blessing of the Goddess (later replaced by her male counterpart, God). She carries the chosen child/ children upon her sacred waters to be received and nurtured by her ambassador or manifestation until the times comes for them to fulfil their destiny. And so, in our story Lupa acts as this Divine Intervention, this affirmation of kingship from the Goddess herself.

And just as each Goddess is the personification of one part of the Great Divine, so each Goddess offers her particular essence to the king she has chosen; Inanna offering her skills and knowledge as Goddess of War and Queen of the Heaven to King Sargon, Moses was found by the daughter of the Pharoah who would have been a priestess of Hathor or Isis, and Cerridwen muse of the Welsh bards and the source of poetic inspiration was the mother of the great bard Taliesin. So then, we have Lupa as Wolf Mother offering to her wards her unique characteristics of ferocity, dedication and confidence. Some people say the first seven years of our life are the most informative in creating our personality, strengths and weaknesses, so imagine being fully immersed in the presence of the divine for these informative years, what greatness would that facilitate?

In addition to this in some versions of the origin story, for example, that written by Titus Livy[6], the twins do, however, also inherit some of their divinity from their parents. Romulus and Remus are descended from a king through their female lineage via their mother Rhea Silvia, a Vestal Virgin[7] and daughter of Numitor, King of Alba Longa, as well as their demi-divineness through their Father who was the God Mars. Nothing but the Mother Goddess truly would be good enough for nursemaid and protector of these children!

The children were 'fated' through their conception and physical birth by their mother Silvia but then they also received their second birth and initiation with Lupa, within her womb-tomb of the cave. As keeper of the birth and death mysteries and acting as the personification of the Mother Earth Goddess she held in her great paws the unfurling of divine timing. Is it really any surprise that after this beginning that Rome went on to become the eternal city and longest Empire the world has known so far?

This importance of this initiation of the twins with the Wolf Mother was later affirmed and also re-enacted with the festival of Lupercalia and the Lupercal rite of running around city from the cave and back again. We see in this festival some sort of remnant of the celebration and remembrance of initiation as given by the Goddess, by the river, in the cave.

The ancient Roman politician Cicero says that while the souls of all men are immortal, those of the good and brave men are divine.[8] Yet before they can even speak Romulus and Remus are set on the road of fate, and arguably pre-ordained divinity. They do not achieve this through their own good works or good character, their destiny was decided before they could even talk. Their initiation comes through the presence of the she-wolf and her breastfeeding them and her taking them to the cave (literally and metaphorically).

Is this perhaps a pre-Roman Etruscan idea of the gods choosing the fate of man rather than the Grecian influence or view of man being able to claim/achieve divinity? We see man-made divinity in the Grecian traditions with Hercules as an example and then is later adapted by the Romans. For example, Augustus makes Julius Caesar divine, but only after his death. This deifying of Julius Caesar was, of course, partly a political move designed to validate Augustus' rulership but also signalled a new belief that you could became a god through your own efforts.

But even if man could become a God through his own action rather than divine designation, lineage from the Great Mother, was still important. Julius Caesar in his lifetime, not only claimed to be a descendant of Romulus, but his true validation was through his claim to be a descendant of Venus. Venus was a very ancient Etruscan deity who was a protectress of vegetation and gardens. She was the woods, the fields, the animals and the flowers.

It is interesting that he made this choice not to claim a descent from Zeus, Mars or even Apollo, but sacred lineage from Venus, the Divine Feminine and Mother Nature. Perhaps even as Rome grew, expanded and changed it still remembered and sought validation from the Goddess, in recognition of her right and importance in offering legitimacy to rule.

Part 3: Rome Grows Up - Lupa in
Ancient Roman Society & Culture

Lupa's central place in the identity of Rome continued well into the time of the Republic and the Empire. Her story become even more famous in the 1st century BCE when the 'Constitution of Romulus' was circulated and her story was revived for political purposes. A little while later Livy's *History of Rome*, written at the time of Augustus, also had its contribution in the She-Wolf being known far beyond the city of Rome itself. Augustus himself, as part of his revival even contemplated renaming himself Romulus, to hint at almost a second coming to the citizens of Rome! Also, like Julius Caesar, Augustus celebrated his ancestry from Romulus and through him his lineage from both Venus and now also Mars.

For the everyday people of Rome, the image and energy of the She-Wolf still held importance. We can see, for example, displays of the belief in the protective qualities of the wolf. Pliny[9] records in Rome's rural districts that on the arrival of a bride to her new home she smeared the doorposts with wolf's fat and oil, and wound fillets of wool around it. The fat of wolf was used as a charm against evil spirits. Only once she has performed this rite could she pass over the threshold and be received by her husband and be symbolically accepted as the materfamilias to her husband.

Pliny, a respected Roman writer, also noted the belief that was still held by the Romans in the 1st century CE, that if an amulet of a wolf's tooth was worn by children it would protect them from nightmares. There have also been found some Bullae's, Roman amulet's given to male children nine days after birth, that has upon them the image of a she-wolf. The Bulla, made of cloth, leather or sometimes gold was worn around the neck as a talisman to protect the young wearer from evil energies. The mortality rate of babies in ancient Roman was exceptionally high. At some periods it was as high as one in two babies dying in their first year of life, and on average one in three children did not live beyond the age of seven. Therefore, it is understandable that they would wish to call on Lupa, the great protector of the infant twins, to also protect their own children and ward off evil just as she has scared of the twins' attackers.

Depictions of Lupa in Roman Life
The most frequent depictions of deities from the ancient world survive for us in artwork.

So let us look at some examples of the symbolism and relevance of the wolf and Lupa for Roman society and art.

One place in which we find frequent depictions of the she-wolf is on coins. Earlier on, she is depicted on her own, as just the she-wolf. Here she is shown as sacred in and of herself and in movement, full with divine milk and ferocity. (see silver denarius 77BC)

Silver denarius, dating to the year 77 BCE,
depicting the she-wolf walking to the left (Crawford 388/1b)

Silver denarius from Rome (45 BCE)

A little later we can see a Silver Denarius from Rome (45 BCE) which has on the back of the coin the two central symbols of Rome: The She-wolf and Jupiter's eagle. Here we see the she-wolf placing a stick either into the fire, adding fuel, or being the one to light the fire itself and the eagle is fanning the flames.

This coin is showing Lupa's role in keeping the fire of the empire or state burning. It is therefore honouring her as the point of creation, the spark of ignition, with the eagle, the symbol of the army and Jupiter, as the vehicle of its growth.

We then in a later coin see her depicted suckling Romulus and Remus. Here she is depicted as sacred in her role and function in relation to the twins and as milk nurse. It is interesting that these depictions of Lupa change with the rise and expansion of the Empire.

Aureus, gold coin, from c.AD 124-128, celebrating Hadrian's 3rd consulship, depicts the she-wolf, suckling the twins Romulus & Remus (RIC II 192)

These coins would have been in the hands of the citizens of not just Rome but the Empire. In this way Lupa's image would have been viewed and handled every day by a large proportion of the estimated 50 to 90 million inhabitants of the height of the Roman Empire. Also, it shows that she is in the fore-front of conscious mind and a figure of importance, with value enough to be depicted on the coins along with the emperors. They would have served as a daily reminder to all Romans of the foundation of Rome and the aspired to energy and essence of being Roman.

We can also find her in visual depictions and representations in Roman art and particularly in the form of sculpture as well as images in mosaics and wall paintings.

These depictions were not only in Rome but the image and story travelled throughout the empire. We even find her roaming around in the U.K with a picture of either a jolly or menacing she-wolf in a Roman mosaic in northern England

She-Wolf with Romulus and Remus. Roman Mosaic from Roman Villa in Aldborough, Yorkshire c.300 CE

As well as the She-Wolf, wolves in general were also depicted in Britain during the Roman period. 'Wolves of Mars' (father of Romulus and Remus) was a bronze figurine of a ferocious wolf devouring a man that was found in the remains of a temple in Oxfordshire, and was made as an offering to Mars.[10] In contrast to Lupa, Mars' wolves are depicted with quite a different character to her maternal care and nourishment. They are always masculine and often devourers and deadly fighters, quite like the God of War himself.

We also find in Yarmouth, a Roman bronze wolf designed to mounted on the top of a religious staff. The sceptre was used in the Roman period as an emblem of power and so this depiction is a reminder to the user of the wolf as a symbol of strength and leadership.

Capitoline Wolf

Bronze statue of the Capitoline She-Wolf in Rome,
5th Century BCE

The earliest attested statue of the she-wolf suckling the twins was by Gnaeus and Quintus Ogulnius in 296BCE (Livy 11-12). Its location was suggested to be nearby to the Lupercal on Palatine Hill but it no longer seems to be in existence.

However, one of the most well-known depictions of Lupa that does remain is the Capitoline Wolf statue, now situated in the Musei Capitolini in Rome. It is a cast bronze statue of a she-wolf suckling Romulus and Remus.

This famous statue is determined to be a pre-Roman Etruscan bronze statue of a she-wolf to which Romulus and Remus were later added in the medieval or renaissance period.

It is only the she-wolf part of this statue that is ancient and she stood alone originally. Romulus and Remus were placed underneath at least a thousand years later when the story had a revival of sorts in Christian Roman era art. So, in this iconic depiction she was originally honoured as HER-self, not just in her role of nurse.

The pointed teeth and jutting ribs of this statue and others of Lupa were meant to portray her ferocity and strength. It is a far cry from other statue art of the later Roman period which celebrated the dynastic and military glories of men, as well as dignified noble faces. In her portrayal she almost always remains Etruscan, with that wild and untamed elemental essence.

At the time of its creation in the c.500's, the high cost of bronze made it accessible only to a few but its popularity resulted in pottery called Bucchero (from the Clusium area) which imitated burnished mental in both polish and colour. The use of such a large amount of high-quality bronze for the Capitoline she-wolf is a tribute to her importance and value to her people. The creation of the statue was an act of devotion.

There were originally many she-wolf sculptures in ancient Rome, as mentioned by contemporaries of the time, so important was this legacy of Lupa. One statue of Lupa is specifically mentioned by the Cicero, an important Roman statesman, philosopher and scholar and contemporary (and rival) of Julius Caesar. It is an interesting incident that he writes about:

...the nurse of Roman dominion, suckling with life-giving dew that issued from udders distended, struck by lightning she toppled to the earth, bringing with her the children, torn from her station as she left the prints of her feet in descending. (Cicero, De Divinatione, 1.20)[11]

By this point Romulus and Remus had already been added to her statue, rather than just her alone. However, even 700 years after the founding of Rome, when Cicero was writing, Lupa was still important. Her story still known and she remained a central figure in Roman life and identity, as shown by the presence of the statue itself in such an important location and the name by which Cicero describes her is one of respect.

I wonder what the Roman people thought of Jupiter's Lightning bolt striking the she-wolf and separating her from her twins, and so severing the link of nourishment and nurturance from Rome itself? Cicero certainly notes that it was auspicious. This event documented by Cicero happened in 65BC. Interestingly at this time the Roman Senate passed the Lex Papia, which expeled all foreigners from Rome, in response to the illegal exercise of citizen rights by foreigners. Yet in its foundation, Rome, if we remember, was a town founded by outsiders, immigrants from somewhere else, seeking and then creating a new home.

Thinking back to the Etruscan beliefs in lightning divination I do wonder whether they would have seen this moment as a symbolic act with a warning attached to remember where they came from? It was well known that the wolf goddess was also the protector of foreigners and ally of those starting anew[12].

The Roman writer Livy also reports in his *Roman History* that a statue of a solitary she-wolf was erected at the foot of Palatine Hill in 295 BCE[13]. Presumably marking either Lupa's cave, or the place in which she found or suckled the twins.

Pliny the Elder mentions the presence of a she-wolf statue in the centre Roman Forum as well. He says that the she-wolf was *"a miracle proclaimed in bronze nearby, as though she has crossed the Comitium[14] while Attus Novius[15] was taking the omens"*.

We can almost imagine from this description her proudly striding across the public meeting space reminding them that this was her place and that though these men made their grand decisions within the walls they had put up, it was all only possible because of her insight, courage and decision to protect rather than destroy.

On a side note, her legacy continues even now in modern depictions. She has most certainly not been forgotten and there is still a pride of the city of this icon and mythological symbol. The she-wolf takes pride of place on many iconic guidebooks to

Rome, music and art festivals, as well as being the image used for the football shirt badge of A.S Roma. Let us next explore more the places and times in which Lupa was celebrated.

For the Romans it was extremely important to mark and remember the deities within the context of their sacred places and times. The Pax Deorum, was the contract of good relations between Romans and the gods and was maintained by humans through festivals and sacrifices and by the gods through signs and wonders. So where was Lupa honoured and how?

Lupercal

The Lupercal was the place that was known by the ancient Romans to be the location of Lupa's cave and located at Palatine Hill. The site remained important to the Roman people and it became a grotto-shrine throughout its history, only to be lost for a while during the last thousand years. The Lupercal was re-discovered by archaeologists this century, just 15 miles away from Augustine's palace. What is left to us now is an underground room or cavern, with vibrant decoration, mostly of a later date than the original structure.

It was because of this sacred location and the events that unfolded here that Palatine Hill became, or remained, the 'royal house'. It became the chosen location for the emperor's palace, which was located next to the hut of Romulus. It was an important reminder of the emperor's connection to his royal lineage and the continued holy heritage of his office.

As part of his 'revival' of Old Roman religion, Emperor Augustus also initiated restoration work and then re-consecrated Lupa's original cave for the festival of Lupercalia. This was one part of his grand scheme which actually included repairing 82 temples. He also brought back a lot of ancient ritual, transformed priestly collages and also elected himself as the head priest of the state *Pontifex Maximus* (Latin for "greatest priest") and made the role an Imperial office.

Interestingly, the Temple of Cybele was also built next to the Lupercal. Cybele was known as 'The Great Goddess' and is believed by some to be the original source or first manifestation of most ancient mother great goddess figures. Lynne Roller argues that the placing of Cybele's shrine next to ancient and important shrines such as the Lupercal and the Hut of Romulus is an indication of the recognition and esteem in which Cybele's cult was held.[16] Only the most holy of holies was deemed worthy of being in this location! Also interesting are the origins of Cybele's name which are believed to stem from the word *Kubaba* which means cave, and the ideograms of her name include a door or gate. Whether this temple was built next to the cave on purpose because of this we cannot be sure, but I like to speculate that in some way a connection was felt between Lupa and Cybele, whether it be as Mothers Goddess' of origin and creation, or as a Goddess of the Cave-Threshold.

We must also add here that the cave was still an important symbol of initiation in the psyche of the Romans. The Lupercalia festival began its yearly run in the Lupercal, which we will discuss later, but also the grotto-cave was noted as important for other Roman religious activities. An example of this is the grotto shrine of The Sibyl of Cumae. This cave was also a place of initiation and the Sybil's, the Priestesses of Apollo, had the gift of prophecy. There is a link here again that emphasises the belief in knowing, hearing or divining one's destiny within the cave. Like Lupa, these Priestesses are of pre-Roman origin, linking back to older rites and practices.

At the entrance to the Lupercal cave on Palatine Hill legend has it that there was also a fig tree. This fig tree was a symbolic aspect of the foundation story and the holy fig tree at the cave entrance became the mother tree to many other sacred fig trees that were planted and used for rituals throughout the city of Rome. We also know that the figs were used in the Lupercalia festival rites at the cave.

We will look in more depth at this symbol of the tree and its relation to the goddess and Lupa's story in Chapter 5, however, it is worth noting here the scaredness of this tree. It was the called the Ficus Navia and it was held to be very important. Pliny notes that *"whenever it died it was taken as an omen and the priests planted a replacement"*.[17] It was seen as auspicious when it died in 58.AD but then it revived and put forth new shoots which was seen as a great sign for Rome!

Lupercalia

It is often said that there was at least two or three festivals or feasts held for a deity every single day in Ancient Rome. However, one of most interesting in relation to our exploration of Lupa and the she-wolf is the annual 'Wolf' festival linked to the priesthood of the Lupercalia.

Lupercalia was an extremely popular festival of purification held annually mid-February. This festival is most often believed to be of pre-Roman origin and had its roots in a more ancient initiation rite. Even Plutarch, writing around the time of 100 CE, was unsure of the origin of the festival, rituals and traditions, so long had they been performed. Perhaps we can speculate that the origins lie again with the pre-Roman agricultural cultures of central Italy.

The festival became ultimately a fertility festival with many links and references to Lupa in its symbology and ritual. This festival was celebrated at a time of new growth and beginnings in nature, for us now just after what we call Imbolc. It does then seem an appropriate time to celebrate, remember and re-create the threshold moment of Romulus leaving Lupa's cave and then later to return to that same spot to create his new city.

In imitation of Romulus the festival involved young, noble men (sometimes said to be just a select two) leaving the Lupercal in just goat skin girdles, running like wolves around the city following a circular route that marks the boundaries of the earliest city, before finally returning to the cave. These young men were for a day literally known as the wolf sons. Along their run was later added the opportunity to whip everyone they met with strips of goat skin so that those people would receive a fertility blessing. To be whipped by these running men was to ensure a conceiving of a strong son. It was also auspicious to birth a son during this festival – he would grow to be like a wolf!

Much of Palatine Hill was opened to the public on this day, including the Lupercal and before they began their traditional lap of the city, the runners underwent a ritual within the cave, involving being marked with blood and milk by the Luperci Priests (Brothers of the Wolf)[18]. The runners had their forehead smeared with blood, which was then wiped off with wool dipped in milk, after which Plutarch says they were obliged to laugh.

The blood was symbolic of the sacred blood line of kings from Romulus and the milk symbolic of the divine breastmilk of Lupa. Some have also suggested that the blood may be symbolic of sacrifice or in earlier times the life-blood of the womb and so of the sacred bloodline of the Goddess herself.

The run was meant to be in imitation and recreation of the run of the founder of the Rome himself, from the legendary cave of the she-wolf, around the hill on which he chose to build his city. His run marked the physical outline for his vision, in reverence of the sacred time and place where he was nursed and raised. It was by tradition a statement of intent and possession but this boundary was also believed to be sacred, containing within it the holy of holies and sanctified ground. Ovid adds that the run marked exactly the sacred boundaries of the ancient city that was marked out by Romulus himself with stones.[19]

Tradition has it that Marcus Anthonis (known to us as Cleopatra's Marc Anthony) famously took part in this festival and his participation was noted and marked as a sign of great things to come from him. Marcus himself also chose this festival to offer Julius Caesar a royal crown, perhaps to test the public opinion on Caesar's potential promotion to King from Senate. This highlights that importance of festival in the remembrance of kingship and initiation. It serves again as a reminder of initiatory rites, facilitated by the divine presence of the she-wolf that Romulus undertook in his journey to destiny. In the foundation story if the twins had just been left at the water without the involvement of Lupa, they would have died. It was the time, their time, within her cave and receiving her milk, that marked them for kingship. Therefore, it was this time, this festival that Marcus chose as the ideal time to openly air the possibility of a new king in Caesar.

She-Wolves of the Lupanarium

When reading about ancient Roman life you will again and again find the word Lupa repeated not in the context of the she-wolf of the foundation myth but in the context of the everyday lives and streets of the Romans. For in ancient Rome's Latin vocabulary, the term Lupa was also a term for a common female prostitute.

For ancient Roman society sex was something that went hand in hand with the power and authority of men. There were, however, some general rules and guidelines for a man in pursuit of his pleasure.

It was neither expected or celebrated for a man to have sexual fidelity to his wife (though for her it was essential to retain her *pudicitia* – her 'chastity'). It was the ideals of Roman piety and dynastic pride that were held to be of most importance. It was often a case of not what a man did, but how it did it. Men of wealth did not generally need to visit brothels because of the availability of slave concubines or mistresses. If a man were to search outside of his marriage for sexual activities it would not be within the upper levels of social class. He would look instead to his slaves, or even sometimes to those of the poorer levels of society. Those within the poorer levels of society themselves who could not afford their own slaves or concubines would turn to the brothels and prostitutes.

The word Lupa was most often used in slang to mean a low-level prostitute and a Lupanar, meaning wolves den, to mean a lower-class brothel. However, in ancient Pompeii the biggest, best planned and most richly decorated brothel is also known as the Lupanarium, meaning 'the wolves lair'. The term Lupa was given in reference to the belief in the prostitute's predatory nature, who would actively ensnare their clients, like a lamb hunted by a wolf.

Historians now estimate that one in every four of prostitutes were slaves and usually of Greek or Eastern origin, there were often very young with no hope of ever leaving their line of work and along with actors and gladiators had many legal and social disadvantages.

As well as offering the obvious services historian T. McGinn shares that these prostitutes were often considered able to support their clients emotionally, as well as physically. The Lupa were in fact expected to offer not just physical and sexual services but also to be kind, pleasant, supportive and considerate, even devoted to boosting the self-esteem of their clients. As well as offering what we might term 'emotional' support the prostitutes were also known to heal wounds and were sometimes called upon to offer some basic nursing skills.

Despite their obviously valuable skills and offerings McGinn tells us that the term Lupa is evidence that:

> the rampant misogyny of Ancient Rome was greatly detrimental to all lower-class woman, as exemplified in their nicknames 'she-wolves'. Upper class Roman men would wilfully identify any lower-class women as prostitute, especially if she worked outside of a house or alongside men.[20]

Already the she-wolf had become tied up with negative connotations, as was sex and freedom for women beyond the purposes of procreation and outside of the confines of marriage. These Lupa, the female prostitutes, were women considered outside the controlled roles of wife, mother or maiden daughter and so named after the wild, untamed beasts of the night. However, as the evidence shows, from their lack of freedom and choice, these women were just as under the control and abuse of the patriarchy as many other women of the time.

There have been suggestions by scholars to confirm that the term she-wolf was chosen for these women as a hint towards the judgement of the predatory nature of the prostitute, reflecting the nature of wolves in seeking out and destroying their prey. We must remember that this terminology did reflect the social and cultural norms of society at the time. However, today we may have different opinions and judgements of those women within those roles and we can certainly be emotionally moved by their lack of choice and authority within their own lives. We may wonder at how many of these women actually had any say in becoming or remaining a prostitute and offer our own opinion on how 'predatory' these women actually were. The freedom of the wild wolf, roaming on her own terms and being able to protect and lead her pack was not something that the Lupa prostitutes could ever even hope to experience.

One of the clear messages that came through from Lupa herself is that as we invoke, work with and celebrate her, we should also feel a deep gratitude and appreciate our freedoms at this time and also take the time to remember and honour those that did not have our current choices when it comes to how and where we work. In reclaiming and honouring our self-authority and the sacredness of our bodies, we are also doing so for those women who could not and did not have full ownership of their bodies or sexuality. You have the ability and opportunity now to choose self-sovereignty, never forget that.

In remembering and celebrating Lupa as Goddess, sacred and holy, we are in fact also contributing to a reclaiming of the word Lupa, and the untamed nature of woman, as not wrong but so very right. Perhaps we can also somehow heal the wound of exploitation and abuse that has been a muzzle for our beloved she-wolf. I believe it is time for the Lupa, the she-wolf, to no longer be a derogatory term used to slander 'uncontrolled' women but indeed a celebration of the potentiality and fierceness of woman.

To Roam Free - The Future for Lupa

The she-wolf played a significant role in Roman myth and culture from the humble beginnings of ancient Rome all the way to the present day. She appears frequently in art, mosaic, story, coinage as well as poetry, political manifesto and military device. Part of her legacy is that she still remains one of the most recognizable icons of ancient European mythology.

There are many stories in reverence to the ancestors, which were central to the creation and maintenance of religious and social life. These legends and myths created identity and belonging for individuals, nations and cultures. We have explored Lupa as vital and contributory in so many different of her different aspects; the untamed Etruscan nature spirit, a fierce and wild protector of the innocent and protector of the defenceless, the mother of courageous and pioneering men and wetnurse to an Empire.

Ancient Rome's religion was essentially pragmatic and utilitarian, involving regulated and structured worship and ritual. We can see within this how Lupa may have become just a temporary milk-nurse to some historians, and yet every time the story is told there will always be references to, and elements incorporated, that remind us of the deeper and more profound aspects of her healing and wisdom.

Despite her much earlier origins in the ancestral realms of the Latins, Etruscans, Villanovans and beyond, Lupa remained at the centre of Roman life and identity, well into the Empire. She even survived, though only as a 'entertaining story', through the period of Christianity into the modern day where she still reigns sovereign in Roman art, culture and entertainment. It is within this context that we see Lupa continue to remain significant as mythical figure, sometimes deity, but always as ally and protective, supportive companion.

In ancient Roman religion there is the idea of the 'Genius'. The Genius was the individual spirit/entity that protected and guided a person throughout their life. Imagine a guardian angel or spiritual mascot for a person or home that would protect from birth to death and thereafter. The term also incorporated the divine nature or essence that was present in each thing, individual and place.

Lupa was the Genius of the forest and the cave, then the twins, before becoming the Genius for Rome, the Empire and all its inhabitants from the Jordan to Scotland. Her icon, image and story, like the wolf roamed far and wide and suckling all that needed her, just as Roman citizenship was open to all free peoples within her empire if they wished it. She was and remains a caring guardian and fierce protector for all those that seek shelter, nourishment and insight in her cave.

The Empire owed its might and power to her in the offering of her breastmilk, whether the literal milk given to its earliest founders, or the milk of inspiration and courage in later times. We also know that the resources beneath the city of Rome's feet is what enabled it to become the power that it did. We need to just look at the waterproof cement created from Rome's earth, the prominent hills offering safety and protection and the access to the Tiber to see that Rome owed its success and thriving ultimately to the gifts of the primal, wild earth Mother, whom Lupa personifies and represents.

Rome went on to be the first city of a million people and each one of them walked upon the mighty paw prints of a she-wolf!

It was her land and offered by her as sanctuary to her human pack. The wolf is even now still the national animal of Italy in recognition of the ancestors of the land.

Lupa, however, does not just offer her guardianship to Rome and the Empire but for all. As Wolf Mother and guardian, she works on behalf of the Wolf Genius. Through the portal of the Empire her form as Lupa became known, and is known, through many lands and peoples. Yet she is also a principal ambassador for the wolf lineage and essence.

Throughout my research of Lupa, I have found that most often historians' comment on the sheer luck or coincidence of the presence of a she-wolf coming to the rescue of two helpless and lost infants and dismissing it as a nice story but unrealistic. However, it we weren't to confine the divine within our own limitations, conditions and judgements, what is possible then?

It is time to reclaim the She-Wolf as her own divine energy, not as a pawn but as a queen. No longer used a piece for larger play and others schemes but perhaps as the most powerful player on the board, able to choose and move in ways that enable, initiate and actualise destiny.

Regardless of gender she invites us to celebrate and embody the wildness, fierce instinct and raw power of the feminine, of Mother and of the untamed woman.

So, if we were *"to dream the dream onwards and give it a modern dress"*[21] what will be the legacy of Lupa's mythos and how can we continue to take it forward?

With respect and remembrance of what has been before, we can connect now to her as modern human beings, in our time, culture, and with our own unique needs and desires. She is a powerful guide to show us the way in reclaiming our inner and outer feminine; to become a fierce, passionate embodiment that knows her path, honours her instinct and intuition and courageously surrenders in full allowance of receiving nourishment and wisdom from the divine.

So, in reflection of this, the second half of this book is an opportunity for you, dear reader, to connect with Lupa is your way, to let her find you at the banks of the river and let her take you on your own unique journey. What remembrance will she offer you when you join her in the cave of transmutation and transformation?

In the next chapter I share a re-telling of the story of Lupa, pulling together all of the threads of research, history, wolf wisdom and intuition but most predominately this is Lupa's essence and energy itself. These are her words, listen deeply.

This has been one of the prominent motivating factors in writing this book; Lupa asked to share her story and perspective, to have remembered her essence beyond and deeper than the intentions and perspectives of the patriarchy of the past, so she can be re-claimed and heard again by her she-wolves and wolf-pack.

For this story I invite you to make this a sacred space and time. Light a candle or incense following the suggestions in the last section of this book and make sure you are comfortable lying down or seated. You can be outside with nature, on the ground or near a river or cave or cosy at home. Take some long, deep breaths before we begin. If you would like to listen to me reading this story to you, you can do so via my website.

Chapter 2

Her-story Re-told

Running, she is the wind and the rain. Running, she is the soil into which she sinks. Running, she is the green of the leaves and the branch as its catches and bends. Running, she is her prey and the moon light that catches on its fur as it turns deeper into the forest. Running, she is every creature, she is the blood pumping, the scent, the breath and the meetings and partings in the dance of life and death.

With hardly a sound or a pause of thought she slows and sinks her body low to the ground, waiting for the forest to return to stillness. She catches the scent of her pack approaching behind her. They wait, her youngest gently whining, restless in anticipation. They are on the hunt and they have been travelling the land throughout the night in search of food.

The forest is still dark but something feels different now, here. She lowers herself closer to the earth and turns her ear to listen deeper. Waiting. Curious. Then she feels it tingle through her bones, tail to crown, like a slow-moving lightning bolt.

It is time.

The scent of different seeps through her being and she knows, it is time. With her knowing she is called away from the hunt and a glance to her mate invites him to take the lead of the pack till her return.

There is something she must do and the sun rises as she meanders through the forest on her own, allowing now only the crunch of fallen, dead leaves beneath her paws to accompany her south.

Emerging from the forest, she gracefully walks over the undulating hills until she looks down upon the river below. With confidence she sets her eye on *the* spot and holding her eyes in intention does not look away until she is there.

At the riverbank she notices the flooding fullness of the river and within her swells the high wave of anticipation. The sun rises over the water, threads of gold and red weaving an ever moving and changing picture. Man may ask why the sun did not rise sooner, but she knows that we all rise only when it is our time.

She feels them and turns her head in welcome. The current shifts. The river meanders and then finally in the distance she sees them. The river offers up a basket and it comes to rest right between her paws. They are smaller than she imagined, not yet skilled in that human ability to make themselves believe they are bigger than they are.

At the ending of that watery, rhythmic flow the babes begin to cry and she lifts them up from the basket, leaving it to flow downriver. They pine, so many tears that they must be as blind as her new born pups. So, with her teeth she pulls away the too tight, wet swaddling. They stop their chorus as she licks away their tears and dirt, they fall into a trusting silence as she soothes their bruises and cuts with her tongue. As she cleans them the babe's now free hands reach up towards her, gripping onto her fur, holding on, anchoring.

Then she smells other. Wrong. Threat. A band of men with spears of ill intent. She stands to block the babes from view, hair rising, chest expanding, she growls. Mine. They are mine to protect. Mine.

They come closer and she barks with all of her power and courage. She is Mother and the men become small in the face of her ferocious love. She scares them away; they retreat to create false tales of bravery and slaughter.

She picks the babes up without delay and carries them up from the marshy bank, up the hill away from danger. Following her path, she reaches the place upon the hill just as the sun is beginning to set. The fig trees protect and cover the entrance, large leaves acting like a canopy to a crib. The last of the fruit on the branches is falling and their juice drips down red to anoint as they pass beneath the bough and pass into the darkness of the cave. She knows this cave well, the sanctuary of mother and pup.

In the cave, her den, she takes the babes to the chamber at the end of the tunnel. Elevated above the damp floor, lined with soft soil, to sets them down to sleep, curving her warm, fur body around them.

When they wake, they see into the dark and know that she is there. When they cry, she suckles them, feeding the hunger, reassuring with presence, offering her body to sleep upon, comfort and peace.

In this time of retreat, their nightmares transform into dreams. As they dream, she watches over them, seeing every movement, hearing every gurgle, knowing every need. Each time when they wake, they look into the darkness and see something new, utter a new sound or move a new way.

As they grow, time and fate weaves itself around them. Her gentle whimpers an ancient lullaby that sings a thread to join with another. Her heartbeat a rhythm of gnosis so they would know and remember.

For as long as it would take, she would stay with them, protect them, nurture them. Surrendered to time, for revelation, restoration, reclamation. She knows that a great destiny lies before them and growth cannot be rushed or the plant grows unrooted. They slept, dreamt and grew until she woke them from their slumber.

For the first time they would go out to play and learn. She would teach them how the land felt, its textures and what was solid and soft so they would know how to build. She would teach them instinct, so they could smell fear, truth, ease and unease, so they could discern and judge men. She would teach them the colours, meanings and directions of animals, birds, fish and insects so they would know where and how to follow tracks and the signs and wisdom of nature. She would mould them ready to be kings of foundation, princes of the earth, builders of new life.

It is time. And so, she births them anew, re-entering the world together, they walk back out. Their hands grab the she-wolf's fur for stability as she navigates them back towards the light. Buds grow in trees, plants emerge and the sun rises again, brighter this time, more whole and complete.

After it was done, a gentle nudge of the nose towards destiny was needed. She set them on their path to next, after. They take their first tentative steps onward, with a few glances behind to remember the Mother who waits and watches, guides and encourages.

As they leave, she howls once to the children and to her pack. Beginning and ending, one and the same. Her sense of smell means that she will always remember them and know them when they return. She would watch them from the outskirts, see them as they chose weapons to channel their ferocity, find the human words for knowing, honour and the sacred and apply their instinct when meeting people, choosing place and time and discerning right from wrong. She will watch them knowing her truth and what she offered even when this was forgotten and lost.

Even many years from then she would remember the smell of someone in need and will welcome them back into the cave. She will know you, sense you, will welcome your return. You will find her waiting at the river's edge, when you are ready.

Running, she is the winds and the rain. Running, she is the soil into which she sinks. Running, she is the green of the leaves and the branch as its catches and bends. Running, she is whole and holy, sacred and sovereign and the moon light catches on her fur as she turns deeper into the forest. Running, she is every creature, she is the blood pumping, the scent, the breath and the meetings and partings in the dance of life and death.

Chapter 3

Teachings of the She-Wolf

Symbology and Deeper Meaning in Her-story

Let's take a deeper look at the symbology and gems of wisdoms contained within the mythology and story of Lupa so that we can understand and know her message within our own souls and hearts. What deeper layers and currents lie beneath the surface of the water, in the darkness of the cave?

Wolf as Mother

Animals are often used to invoke particular qualities or attributes associated with a particular deity. The animal chosen was the one that best represented that deities' particular powers, inclinations, characteristics or offering, such as the eagle for Jupiter and the Goose for Juno. So why a she-wolf in the foundation story of Rome and why a wolf to suckle the twins?

As we have explored already is our previous chapters, wolves were well known to our ancient ancestors, both as strong and ferocious protector. Other characteristics that wolves are known for are fierce intelligence, courage and endurance. Wolves are also well known for their devotion to their pack and the mutual support and loving companionship shared between the members of their family. They will defend this family and especially their cubs to their last breath. They often seem without fear and use their high instinct and intuition to know when and how to act, in the dark and in the daylight alike. For anyone that has been near a wolf you can see just how deeply clever they are and how they will sense and smell you physically and energetically long before you even know they are there. They nurture, play and are loyal, all of which is still clearly displayed in their descendants that offer invaluable contribution as our everyday pet dogs.

So, who better to have as the twin's mother, for them to emulate the characteristics of? If you were to choose a king or queen how many of the above characteristics would be in your tick list?

As a symbol and an archetype throughout history warriors are often likened to wolves because of many of these qualities. Yet the mother aspect of the she-wolf adds an extra dimension to the fierce and strong warrior. It gives the warrior the energy of discernment rather than thoughtless attack, the motivating fire of passion and heart led cause, rather than careless action and steadfast, courageous nurturance rather than destruction.

The she-wolf is also intimately connected to the cycles of life and death, through her roaming of the night in the wild hunt and her season-synced pregnancies. She is also associated with death-rebirth in her connection with the cave, symbolically the womb-tomb, which we will explore in more depth in a little while. In this aspect she offers us an ally when we explore our own subconscious and shadow self.

When we are giving death to falsity that fierceness and courage of the wolf is essential. When there are places that we fear to go, especially within ourselves, that needs the energy of the warrior or warrioress, the wolves can facilitate embodying this. Lupa is the mother of this stripping away of all that is no longer aligned or resonate so you can be who you are truly meant to be and embody your essential self of truth. She is a guardian of alchemy that will support you in turning base metal into gold, that is, your woundings and fears into gifts and purpose. When Romulus and Remus were found by Lupa, it was destiny. A certain colour of thread was being woven into their tapestry of life and all other possible paths would just not fit or match anymore. After leaving the cave Romulus could never be a farmer or a travelling musician without feeling unfulfilled. Something had been awakened in him that could not be satisfied by anything other than leadership, creation, power.

The wolf also symbolises the wisdom of the ancients, the she-wolf is one of our spiritual allies that has been with us since the beginning of humankind. Part of you will remember when we walked side by side with wolf, in the physical and dream land and longs to do this again. That is why you are reading this book!

The she-wolf is a powerful archetype for any woman or man to embrace and embody. She reminds us how to protect those we love, when and why to stand our ground and to ferociously align with our truth and protect our sacred boundaries, whether they are sexual, spiritual, emotional or physical.

Being Suckled by the Divine Mother

One of the most important elements of Lupa's story is her choice to breastfeed the twins. Without her nourishment the children would have died. This action, however, was both physical, providing vital sustenance to maintain life, and also symbolic and spiritual. As we know, a mother in breastfeeding does not just offer her milk as food but her reassurance of safety and her presence as a comfort, an emotional and spiritual place to come home to so that one can surrender and receive.

Often when Lupa is mentioned in historical accounts the most central action that she is attributed with is simply, 'she suckled the twins'. That this is the aspect chosen to be mentioned shifts the entire focus of much mythos to her divine role of nursemaid and emphasises the importance of the feminine ability to nurture, nourish and give life.

In this central act of the divine sons receiving the breastmilk of the Goddess Lupa, her connection to the Great Mother archetype is highlighted and her role as a fertility goddess affirmed. Within other cultures, belief systems and traditions, we find similar stories where we are reminded of the importance of sacred breast milk from the Goddess herself (of which the physical milk from any female is symbolic of). In Egypt, for example, we have the Goddesses Hathor and Bata who are celebrated for their breastfeeding roles.

In Egypt we see Hathor as the Celestial Nurse nursing the Pharoah and as this aspect she is often depicted as a cow or sycamore tree. Just like Lupa's Fig Tree, Hathor's Sycamore tree also has a milky juice or sap which was revered and used as if it were the milk of the Goddess herself.[22]

The breasts are the source of life power and the life-giving fluids of the Divine Mother. The flowing breast is also an image of trust in the universe and the divine. The act of Goddess taking a human to her breast also affirms a sense of belonging, an unbreakable bond between Divine Mother and child. In a pyramid text Hathor emphasises this by saying *"Take my breast that you may drink so you can live again"*.

In our story the twins are vulnerable, lost and endangered but in returning to the breast of the Mother Goddess they are once again safe and supported. The inclusion then of Lupa being milk nurse to the two boys significantly hints at a universal theme of the divine mother feeding the divine child on both a physical and spiritual level.

Through the breastmilk the divine child would also receive an aspect, magic, essence or characteristic of the Mother. To be breastfed by Hathor, the Pharaohs of Egypt were gifted with her great benevolence and ability to alleviate all suffering, skills in diplomacy and her all in-compassing joy. Lupa the she-wolf likewise brings and gives her ferocity, courage, leadership skills and sharp instinct to the twins.

Interestingly the sacred fig tree, The Ficus Ruminalis that stood at the entrance to Lupa's cave was later called so in remembrance and celebration of Lupa's choice to suckle the two babies beneath its shelter. The tree was named after Diva Rumina, a goddess who protected breastfeeding mothers and nursing infants. It was Lupa's great act of rescue and nourishing that was honoured by this dedication.

In a translation of Roman Questions (Part of a collection of manuscripts called *Moralia*, attributed to Plutarch) from the 1st or 2nd Century it is asked:

Why do the women that sacrifice to Rumina pour milk over the offerings, but make no oblation of wine in the ceremony?[23]

And the answer was that if it was breastmilk that Romulus himself received then that was ultimately the best Wine, though the most popular offering used in almost all other rituals to deity, was an inadequate substitute as offering in this case. Only milk itself was of unique purity, unaltered through any act of man but still in its form direct from the Mother and this nourishment could be given by the Goddess alone.

The River Tiber

Another important aspect of Lupa's story is the river. Water is the one element that experts universally agree represents life, the feminine, renewal and unconscious mind – where our deepest feelings and emotions reside. Rivers evoke the feeling of time passing, a journey from beginning (mountain) to the end (sea) that symbolises the course of life.

The river is also a threshold, as transitionary place and the river acts as boundary from this world or state to another. For Romulus and Remus their initiation and transition from child to become the founders of Rome takes place following their river journey. Both child and wolf receive from the river a re-directive flow towards the path of divine purpose.

The river can also be symbolic of actually overcoming an obstacle which allows one to reach the next stage of a journey. For Romulus and Remus, the obstacle was being threatened and persecuted as heirs of the old 'regime'. Their journey was to overcome this and become the founders of a new kingdom. The river acted as a bridge of the before and after, carrying them away from Alba Longa to Lupa. They were in a way cleansed by the sacred waters of their old life before and the past was washed away.

It is important that it is Lupa that is guardian of this place, the symbolic river of transition, transformation and transmutation. It is here at the riverbank that she is waiting, watching, ready to receive you and guide you onwards during your own journey also.

It is not mentioned in historic accounts how or why Lupa found the twins on the riverbank of the Tiber. In my story I had her waiting at the riverbank as this is where she showed herself to me. A river bank represents safe ground, a place to contemplate, with confidence or anxiety, on the waters of the inner self. On observing Lupa at the riverbank she was calm and assured in her path and her role, she knew what she was there to do and that she would do it well. She is a potent example to us of being fully surrendered and confidently embracing of her destiny.

The ancient Greek and Roman did actually diefy rivers, portraying them as 'old men' or a personfication of a local masculine god. There are in fact some remote places in Italy where you can still find Roman statues of these river gods. Their depiction of an old and bearded man was symbolic of the wisdom of the Sage or wise man archetype. There is something wonderful about this that I see as the divine masculine as guardians and protectors for the sacred feminine and her flowing waters.

Lastly, in many mythoi the situation of being found in the water itself marked one as from another place, or as a blessed being who was significant or important. The inclusion of the river marks them as belonging to, or marked by a higher being, special, destined for greatness. Similar examples are such as Taleisin and Moses who are also found on a river or riverbank in their mythologies and went on to be inspired leaders with a life-long connection and communion with the divine.

Fig Tree

To the Romans the fig tree was a sacred tree with symbolic importance. In Rome, it was considered an emblem of the future prosperity of the city and Roman people. This is not surprising given its vital role within the story of Lupa and its association with the nursing, protection and breastfeeding of Romulus, its founder.

The most significant tree was Ficus Ruminalis, which was a wild fig tree that had religious and mythological significance in ancient Rome, as it stood near Lupa's cave known at the Lupercal at the foot of Palatine Hill.

In some mythoi it was also within the roots of a Rumina Fig Tree that the floating cradle of Romulus and Remus landed at on the banks of the river Tiber. Ovid, the Roman Poet, also calls this the Romulan Fig Tree and said that parts of this tree still remained during his time of writing.[24]

In some versions of the myth as well as landing at the foot of the fig tree and a fig tree being present at the opening to the cave of the she-wolf, oftentimes Lupa is said to have suckled the babies directly beneath the shelter of the fig tree before taking them to her cave. This I believe it could also be an important repetition of the image that we see many, many times in ancient depictions of the sacred hound guarding the tree of life, the tree representing the Goddess herself and the hound as her guardian, protector and representative. Also, the basket within which Romulus and Remus were cast was said to have been made from the roots of the fig tree. Therefore, the importance of the fig tree and its role as a divine component of the story cannot be denied.

In Ancient Roman life the fig was recognised as full of nutrients and due to its diverse uses in cooking, the fig was an important and common food in the diet of the ancient Mediterranean populations. It may be for this reason that they were present in many myths and legends. The fig was an ever-present part of everyday life and were truly considered a gift from the gods.

It has even been argued that:

> *Because of the association with Romulus and Remus legend, fig trees were looked upon as sacred trees and they were especially venerated by the shepherds. Hence, the use of the fruit to fatten animals may have had a ritual meaning.*[25]

Also, Fig juice was widely employed in Roman religious ceremonies.

In my work Fig Flower and Tree Essence is one that I use frequently in sessions with clients. Fig Tree Essence is a powerful ally for various aspects of mystical healing and reclamation. It encourages an alignment with and bringing forth of truth within any circumstance that has been cloaked in societal, religious or familial stories. When taken it will support you in a remembrance of truth and the noble aspects of yourself will be brought forward. It will help you to feel empowered and enabled to always find the gold in situation and people. It is a wonderful essence therefore for embodying your king or queen aspect.

We can see this essence and the soul-purpose of the fig as a potent collaborator with Lupa as the Mother of Destiny and an empowering healing tool for Romulus as he arrives at his destiny as Father of a City and Empire.

The Cave

We need only to look at the cave art of the Palaeolithic age to know the importance of the cave in both ritual and the psyche of humankind. To our palaeolithic ancestors the cave was a sacred place, and the home of the Goddess. When one entered a cave, you would be entering inside the body of Mother Earth herself. This journey into the realms of the Mother, that which is both within and below, took you to the centre, the beginning and the end, and that which is the womb of life and death. The act of entering into an internal shape and hallowed out space, would have been symbolic of the entry into her womb-tomb (death) before then returning back out, going into life (birth/ re-birth).

In Lupa's myth her cave is symbolic of the Womb of Mother Earth. She takes the twins to the cave-womb so that they can be initiated and reborn again. Lupa as an embodiment of the divine feminine, facilitates their time within the womb-tomb nurturing and nourishing them in preparation for their re-entry into the human world. She is there specifically as a guide because this initiation is to transmute vulnerability into courage, uncertainty into purpose, being adrift into destiny. Her qualities and attributes make her a potent guide for this journey within.

An initiation happens for the twins in the descent into the cave. As they are carried into the dark, they descent into the place of transmutation. It is there in the darkness, both literally and metaphorically, that they partake of the nourishment of the divine, receiving what is necessary for their transformation and then onward journey.

Life, as evidenced in the seasons, menstrual cycle and moon, is an endless cycle of endings and beginnings. You may enter the cave of letting go or dark phase within your own life and how you enter and what you experience there is valuable and often necessary. The surrendering to this death and rebirth process with grace and courage is a choice and a powerful choice and one that Lupa will guide you in if you ask. She was their guide and will be with you also.

We may experience this descent and ascent journey many times in our lives. When you do notice it as an invitation into the womb, through the death and rebirth portal. When we are taken to a place of initiation, transformation and change in our lives, it is here that we learn to surrender and trust and become like a child again; to see with new eyes and to discover what is needed now of ourselves and our purpose in this next phase.

Conclusions

Myth and symbolism are divine instructions and wisdom you re-member and re-awaken from within. All that I have shared with you above is not new, but known by you deep within you. This story is your story.

It is not that the divine is everywhere: it is that the divine is everything[26]

The divine is the she-wolf, the river, the fig, the cave, the Divine speaks through all, each has a sentence of the story to share and I hope by exploring these symbols within the mythos you can feel them on a deeper level within your psyche, heart and soul.

As well as healing mediums within themselves, the symbolic gems are here within the story as signposts, taking you to points and paths of revelation. What have been revealed for you? What resonates and stirs a question, a remembrance and enlightenment?

When you journey with Lupa you will be asked to let go of everything that is not aligned, to step into and become all that you truly are. The boys needed to return to the pause, the womb, the cave, the place between life and death. They experienced life before and life after, a rebirth with the wolf as their new mother. We must enter that same space to remember and then embody our own unique destiny and purpose. It is an initiation that we often fear or resist and most often it seems safer or easier to stay in the known, to stay small, to stay comfy. The binds that keep up seemingly safe and comfy, however, can also keep up bound and limited.

What if you were to be Wolf and take yourself to the cave, the unknown and trust in the unfolding and the process? Ask for Lupa to go with you as guide, guardian and teacher. You have one powerful and loving protector to help you draw on courage, discernment and wisdom as you do so.

Chapter 4

Sacred Tools and Practices for Connection

Lupa as a Guide, Guardian and Protector

The Goddess Lupa is an ally and guide to teach you trust in your path and purpose and to courageously surrender to the divine and your knowing self. She is a powerful mentor for learning self-resourcing and belief, and embodying the power of the feminine to create, manifest and nourish.

She is a Goddess of Threshold: She will help you in getting comfortable with beginnings and endings and in remembering that these two scared gates are one and the same and sacred points of initiation. As wolf she holds the power of life and death in her paws, to destroy or to nurture and so she is also an ally when we need to apply discernment. Listen to your intuition, what is calling you now in the present? What do you need to surrender to or what to do need to allow to pass by? Is there something you need to embody as you sit at the river's edge, courage or patience perhaps? What boundaries need to be asserted or established? What do you need to let go of in order to come into alignment with your truth and be able to step forward on the next stage of your path?

Goddess of Growth: Lupa as the Goddess Luperca was venerated as the giver and supporter of life. She could bestow prosperity and fertility to crops and animals and as the twins grew to be strong and brave under her loving care, so she can support you in the flourishing of self, identity and holistic abundance. Call on her when you need to make that decision about what to keep giving your precious time and energy time to. She also reminds you that life is circular not linear. She-Wolf returns to her cave every winter for the time of pregnancy, birth and nursing. She knows when to return and takes herself within the cave to honour that time and space, giving herself the safety and the security needed to birth, to renew herself and to nurture growth.

She is Goddess of Transformation and Transmutation: She will be with you if you need to travel to the great below, into the womb-cave or are experiencing change in your life. Call on her to be with you during times of transformation and journeying through the inner realms, she can offer insight and guidance. She also reminds you to ask whenever it gets dark, what cave of initiation have you been guided into? Will you be willing to receive in this place, rather than resist? What if you didn't need to struggle or muddle through? What is there was always an ally waiting to hold you and guide you? She reminds you that her cave is not a place to fear that you will be devoured, but that when you enter with honesty, allowance and integrity you will transmute fear to courage, pain to power. Lupa teaches us that is ok to be in the darkness, sometimes it is even essential.

She is a Goddess of Courage: She fought those that would cause the twins harm, displaying the fierceness of the Wolf Mother. Where and how do you need to stand up for yourself or a cause, internally or externally? Call on her when you to need to speak clearly and stand your ground for your truth. She reminds you that you are valuable and worthy of care and honour and it is a courageous act to nourish and love yourself. I share all the time with my students and clients my absolute favourite quote, that has guided me throughout my life; *"courage is not the absence of fear, but the belief that something is more important than it."* Be Wolf, and run confidently through the forest, knowing you are the trees, the winds, the soil. You are all that is life, sacred and capable.

She is Protector and Guardian: The Romans believed Lupa brought the power to bring death to enemies or protection to those under her care. The She-wolf was and is a fierce protector, and as she-wolf she embodies this protective role with maternal care-giving and unconditional love. She is ready and willing to be your Great Protector and Guardian. She will keep you safe and guard you as her own pup. She saved the lives of Romulus and Remus, not only through rescuing them from the water, but also in feeding them and letting them suckle. No matter how lost or threatened you feel, she is there. Let this mythos confirm that in your being. You may want to ask her to protect your space, your energy, your home, self or especially your children. She can also stand guardian and teacher to your inner-child.

She is Mother of Destiny: Lupa will support you in remembering and embodying your life's purpose, just as she did with the twins. She reminds you that all that has been has led you to this very moment now. Nothing was a mistake, but all made a contribution to who you are and who you will become. Your path is unique and you have a purpose that is designed for you alone. On your path of fulfilling and enjoying your purpose she will help you to use discernment, to trust your intuition and to use your initiative. The twin's destiny lay with the Wolf Mother and she can support you in remembering, and embodying your divine purpose, offering you guidance with decisions and choices. In the mythos the baby twins symbolised an emerging consciousness, a time that is yet to come, a time that is midwifed in by a fierce but careful mother that is devoted to her young. She is there for on you when you choose and grow into your new or affirmed ways of being that come with aligning with your truth and purpose.

Lupa is at the riverbank or at the entrance to the cave waiting for us to remember, to reclaim our unique embodiment and path. Here is not the stereotypical perfect goddess, shiny feathers, golden hair and sexy pout that we often compare ourselves with, but the true perfection of the divine feminine that is that which we judge as the 'imperfection' of ourselves. She is the wild, untamed, perhaps lost parts of ourself that need our love and compassion. She is the ferocity and courage that is required to go to the places you fear most and be that which you know is right and true for you. She is those howls in the dark that come from your hunt of that which truly and honestly nourishes and supports your sacred self. Your life is a living legacy and together with Lupa as a guide you will create a new living legacy where your inner and, or outer feminine is not feared or shunned but honoured, untamed, unbound and empowered.

Lupa is wanting now to come forth to weave with you your destiny and purpose, that which no one else but you can contribute and embody. Your unique frequency is a call to the wild and hearing she emerges from the forest.

She is your very own She-Wolf, Wolf Mother and Protectress.

How to Connect with Lupa through Her Sacred Object and Symbols

Here are symbolic items, sacred tools and objects that may support you in your connection to Lupa. You may want to have them with you anytime that you connect to her and her story. They will deepen your connection to her energy and mythos.

Her Sacred Names

Lupa; She-Wolf, Wolf Mother, Guardian of the Eternal City, Holy West Nurse, Protectress of the Young, She of the Cave of Destiny, Lupa Romana, August She-Wolf, Nurse of Roman Domina, Goddess Luperca.

Appearance

Feminine She-Wolf.

Most often appears as a white wolf, but also sometimes a grey-brown wolf, with red, gold or blue eyes.

(It seems that it is her male counter-parts that mostly appear as black wolves)

Students of mine have reported that she often appears to be glowing blue, or with a strong blue aura, when we work with her. I have also found her to have a golden, queenly glow. She sometimes also appears pregnant or with breasts full of milk.

Sacred Colours

Gold, Brown, Grey, White, Bronze, Blue. You may want to wear these colours in your clothing or sacred decoration.

Stones & Crystals

For cleansing, protection and grounding.

Bronze, Labradorite, Clear Quartz, Amethyst, Black Tourmaline

Lupa was the patron Goddess of Bronze.

Element

Primary: Earth (Earth Goddess).

Secondary: Water.

Flora

Figs, Fig Leaves, Fig Blossom, Fig Tree.

Also, wild fig known as 'goat fig'.

I invite you to plant one in your garden so you have your own organic figs and leaves for use.

Food and Drink

Fig juice, figs, milk (goat milk was used in some ancient Roman rituals). During the Lupercalia festival wool was soaked in milk and then used to cleanse the skin. If you have any spare, breastfeeding mothers may also want to offer some sacred breastmilk to the earth in gratitude and blessing.

Mola Salsa

The ancient Romans used Mola Salsa, 'Bread for the Gods' as an offering, upon sacrificial animals, as well as on the altars and into the scared fire. It was made by the Vestal Virgins and combined flour and salt. You may want to make some and sprinkle in a sacred fire like the Romans, or use it as an offering at any of the sacred locations recommended.

Incense and Oils

- **Cinnamon Incense** – Cinnamon was used as an incense by the Romans at funerals. Use the incense when you are working with Lupa within the womb-cave time of letting go all that no longer serves or is no longer in alignment. From every death comes a re-birth and cinnamon will honour Lupa as a threshold Goddess.
- **Saffron, Myrrh and Frankincense Incense** were also frequently used by the Romans.
- **Rosemary Essential Oil** – Lupa's favourite! To aid clear thinking, recollection and enhancement of memories, bringing clarity of inner and outer vision. Also, it can be used for cleansing space and promoting prosperity. Use in an oil burner, for massage, anointing or offering.

Flower & Tree Essences

- **Fig Tree Essence** is powerful for many aspects of the healing and reclamation of yourself as whole and sovereign. It is an incredible ally for bringing forth truth of any circumstance that has been cloaked in societal, religious, or familial stories. It will support you embodying a noble character that can see and celebrate the sacredness in all things.
- **Olive Tree Essence** helps to embody your King essence that is within (whether man or woman). We often ignore

our inner authority but this essence will remind you of the wisdom that is held within so that you use it as a tool for sacred service. Embodying your regal self will also help you to actualise and offer self-validation to your dreams. The King holds dominion and sovereignty over his life (both his inner state and the way in which he serves) and this Essence will invoke that. Olive tree essence will also help you to connect to the lineage of the Great Kings.

- **Walnut Tree Essence** is especially helpful for times in your life when roles/patterns that have been taken on subconsciously or consciously are ready to be shifted and transformed. Walnut Essence helps make a graceful and easeful transition from what has been familiar to what will be most empowering for you.

Candles
- Brown for grounding.
- Black for protection and stability.
- Blue for forgiveness, calm and communication.
- Gold for sovereignty and honour.

Astrology
Could be associated with the Moon – through her divine feminine aspect and wolf night time association but not specifically a moon goddess such as Luna or Selene.

The star Adhara ~ The root chakra star in the constellation of Canis Major (The Big Dog)

Jupiter (planet). Jupiter is the fairy godmother of the cosmos. Known to the ancients as 'the great benefic' it is associated with abundance, growth, expansion, wisdom and magnification. You may want to follow Jupiter's progress and work with Lupa during Jupiter's transits.

Allies

Other associated deities with whom you may want to ask to work in collaboration with Lupa

- **Rumina** ~ Roman Goddess of Breastfeeding and Childcare ~ Together they will help you with tending, caring for and working with children or inner child work and nurturing the child within.
- **Lupercus** ~ God of farmers and harvest ~ For fertility and health of the land and to bring prosperity and manifestation of a project in collaboration with the land or nature.
- **Romulus** ~ When the warrior or king within needs to be called on and embodied!
- **Mars** ~ Roman God of War ~ 'The Strider' ~ Together they offer a collaboration of sacred feminine and masculine for protection. Lupa will help you to intuitively discern boundaries or the self-authority needed and Mars will give you the fire in enforcing it.
- **As Goddess Luperca**, she was deified wolf and was allied with her male wolf consort Lupercus, who was himself identified with the god Pan. Pan has frequently been found observing from the side lines or running alongside during my wolf journeys into the forest. Do not be surprised if you find him there also.

Sacred Time

Wolf Moon January

Also called the old moon. 1ˢᵗ full moon of the Gregorian calendar (in January) and the full moon nearest Imbolc (Celtic festival of new life). The moon is a potent time to let go before you start anew. Called the wolf moon because wolves were heard howling at this time. They would howl as communication between the pack, sometimes long distances, while hunting.

15ᵗʰ *February and Lupercalia*

Often, we cannot (or some would argue should not) celebrate the festivals in the same way the Roman's did. It is not practical, nor kind in our modern judgement, to be running around whipping people or sacrificing goats and dogs, as was required as part of the ancient proceedings of the Lupercalia.

So, in this light, here is a suggestion for celebrating this festival in a new, modern way:

Make a symbolic journey of a walk or run through the woods, perhaps start at a river and visit a cave along the way. Alternatively, you may want to make a symbolic journey to your physical place of birth or the place you experienced an initiation or pivotal life lesson.

While on your journey reflect and perhaps journal on how you have grown, what you have learnt, the trials, obstacles, themes and celebrations of your life.

You could make an offering of milk or fig juice at the home, cave or river (*to return, in gratitude the nourishment and nurturance we've been given, back to the earth*), or consume the milk/juice yourself after using one of the devotionals given in the next chapter (*in symbolic receiving of nourishment and nurturance of body, mind or spirit*).

27ᵗʰ *August*

Roman festival of Volturnalia dedicated to Volturnus 'God of the waters' who later was identified as God of the river Tiber. This would be a good date to make your water blessing or to visit a riverbank. You may want to listen to the either of the recorded journeys while you are there!

Sacred Places

Rome was and always will be, her city. It is in Rome that to this day you will find her image and essence present in ancient and modern works of art, sculpture, advertising, politics and culture.

Palatine Hill

The Lupercal, is the cave in which Lupa gave sanctuary to her adopted sons and suckled them. It was traditionally said to have been a cave at the foot of the hill, under neath a grove of oaks and with springs of water welling up under the rocks. It was recorded that in Emperor Augustus's reign a preserved historic grotto at this location was near collapse. A few times it was 'restored', including during his reign but archaeologists are not definitely sure what was originally there, perhaps a shine to Lupa. Romulus's hut was also 'kept' preserved nearby for some time of Rome's early years.

The Lupercal was located at the south-west foot of the Palatine Hill and was rediscovered by archaeologists in 2007. It was 16m under the ground and they found it to be decorated with marble, shells and mosaics.

At the time of writing due to health and safety reasons the cave is not accessible to the general public. However, you can get very close and still visit the palaces and temples on Palatine Hill!

If you can't make a visit to Palatine Hill in person, you can still visit it in your dreams or meditations, as we do in my online Wolf course.

The River Tiber

If you are looking for the spot of the riverbank where the basket containing Romulus and Remus was found by Lupa then head for the Temple of Hercules. According to tradition the spot is near the Roman-Greek temple dedicated to Hercules Victor, located in the area that was the Forum Boarium (cattle market). The temple is the oldest marble building in Rome built in the 2nd Century BCE and there is a lush garden (and fig trees!) here in which you could connect with Lupa.

I invite you, if you do visit Rome, to offer a water blessing to the Tiber at any part in which it is safe to do so along the riverbank!

From Anywhere in the World

If you cannot visit Rome connect with Lupa at and within a cave, cave entrances, at the banks of the river, or a Fig Tree Grove. Perhaps plant a fig tree in your garden with the sacred crystals suggested at its base. There are also many places within Europe and North African where you may want to also connect with an Ancient Roman site and reflect on legacy, destiny and creation.

Lupa will come and find you whichever location you decide, after all, all roads lead to Rome!

Devotional Invocations

You may want to say something to Lupa when you are connecting to her or would like some words to speak when asking for her help and support with a particular matter. So here are some invocations I have created to support you in this.

You can just read them and absorb the energy and essence, but for most potency I invite you speak them out loud as part of a ritual. You may want to use these once as part of a ceremony or you want to repeat as a daily affirmation.

For when you need an ally or guide in the darkness of the cave

In the darkness of the cave, I call on you She-Wolf.

Please bless me with your sacred presence as I navigate that which seems uncertain and unknown.

The darkness can sometimes seem overwhelming,

Guide me in trusting my instinct in the darkness.

Help me to see with the eyes of the wolf.

To see that the darkness is not empty but contains a seed of hope that with nurture will grow.

I see now that my intuition is heightened in the dark.

Here I KNOW.

And this only strengthens with your support.

I ask to see what lies beyond the conditions and judgements I have chosen that have made this situation wrong, or bad, or scary.

What could I choose now that would bring me ease and joy? I acknowledge that this cave is a chrysalis and in the dark, I align with my truth.

It is my unease that shows me what is not in alignment. I give thanks for this gift.

I trust that I am just at the threshold of something new.

Life is full of endings and beginnings,

What needs to be shed, I shed now,

What need to be let go, I let go now,

What need to be removed to make space for the new, I remove now.

I am wild and free,

Courageous and true.

I am gatekeeper, cavewalker, I am the end and the beginning. I am creation and destruction.

I am pure potentiality and I choose . . . . (*you may want to enter your own word here or just say I choose*)

I choose.

This you are and this I am and so it is and so it will be. Blessed be and thank you.

For support with living your life's purpose and embodying your destiny.

Lupa, Mother of Destiny,

As a humble apprentice/ student to my wolf Genius I willingly ask to remember my unique destiny.

Within me are the codes of stars, and galaxies and I open my body as a vessel for all that is possible now.

I ask,

For the reclamation of my dreams, those I carry and the revelation of those I have forgotten,

For your guidance as I return to the womb of the mother, returning to her for re-alignment.

For teachings and guidance only known and received in the cave, the forests, the stream and the sky.

I surrender the ways in which I have decided what should be, And in courageous release and transmutation, I instead choose what could be, with full allowance and trust.

I am as a child, again, willing to learn, to grow, to listen.

Help me to openly receive nourishment from the flow of divine milk,

So that I may reach my full potentiality.

I act in loving self-compassion every step towards my destiny and I chose to live on purpose.

I also acknowledge that in honouring my unique truth and manifestation, I honour nature and the divine also.

Help me to be, embody, and express who I was born to be for the benefit of the world, of humanity, of time, of the cosmos. Now is the time.

I am ready so make sacred commitment to live in devotion to this path.

And so it is, so it will be. Thank you.

For when you want to call on the fierce protection of the Mother.
(You can modify this devotional to intend it for someone or something else. For example, you could add a child's name to 'I ask for protection for . . . now'.)

Great Guardian Lupa,

I ask for your protection now.

I ask that I know and feel the strong, steady love of your being and essence,

Surrounding me, above, below, within and without.

I ground my roots deep down into the earth,

And I stand, confident and safe with you at my side, under the great fig tree.

I also call on my wolf brothers and sisters,
My pack, tribe and council that has highest intention at its core.
I ask you to surround me and guard the boundaries which I put in place now.
In your presence,
I am reminded that I am not alone.
I am not alone.
I am supported.
I am protected.
And my body, mind and soul are safe.
With my breath now I release any fear and anxiety within me.
I am whole and holy and protected by the fierce love of the mother herself.
Here, now, I feel peace within the mighty guardianship of you, my Wolf Mother.
And so, it is.
I honour you and thank you.

Conclusions and Author's Note

Before I begin my historical research, I always first connect in with the pure essence of energy I wish to channel. Before I form opinions or perspective, and most definitely before I read anyone else's, I journey and connect to what it is that wants to be revealed, shared and offered at this time from the Divine.

It was here in my journeys to meet Lupa that I have often found myself within a cave with whom I call 'Grand Mother Wolf'. She sits by the fire with her wolf cap and shawl, long grey hair, painted face and piercing wolf eyes. Often Lupa took me to her and it was within Lupa's paws, or curled up next to her large, warm wolf body, that I would receive the wisdom ready to be offered by Grand Mother Wolf. I believe they are both part of the sacred lineage of the wolf and the family of the Wolf energy and essence that goes way back and beyond the history of Rome (though, of course, it is Lupa's energy that in this instance has predominately come forth to guide and support you). It was Grand Mother Wolf that put forward the guidance to research Etruscan and Neolithic wolf history deeper and look for foundations and origins there. I am humbly grateful for her guidance and wish to give my thanks here in writing.

For those that are interested in connecting with The Grand Mother Wolf, I invite you to head over to my website and enjoy a free guided meditation, created just for you, where I will take you on an audio journey to receive her wisdom and healing. You can find it at www.wolfwomanrising.com

There are always more layers of unknown history than there are known, that lie far deeper than the small amount that is written or survived but I hope this provides an introduction for you to Lupa and her wisdom and healing.

Let me know how you get on. I would love to hear about your experiences and revelations!! Connect with me on Instagram or join our Wolf Cave Group to share and chat with my Wolf Woman Rising Community. From both myself, Lupa and the wolf mothers, thanks for reading and many blessings for your continued path with her! May your journey with the wolves be one of joy, devotion and a true home coming.

Much love, Rachel xx

About the Author

For those of you that may be interested in my background! I am a glittery and very fluffy variety of wolf that lives and roams in North Wales. I read History with Religious Studies (BA Honours) at university and then went on to complete post-graduate qualifications in History and Heritage Management. I have also worked in the heritage sector for over a decade, primarily working with children, in learning and interpretation and I can claim to have worked in five different castles!

My desire has always been to create a bridge between history and spirituality, to give knowledge a sacred purpose, transmuting it into embodied wisdom and a tool of healing, empowerment and awakening for women. And so, running parallel to my love of history I am also a sacred dance teacher, storyteller, priestess and women's empowerment coach and flower essence practitioner. As well as Wolf Woman Rising, I am also the founder and principal teacher of Under the Dancing Tree School of Sacred Dance. I teach sacred dances including Belly Dance, Polynesian dance, movement meditation and facilitate various mediums of healing dance such as Inner Dance, Awakened Belly Dance and Elemental Dance.

Using my own journey and over 20 years' experience of teaching and training I infuse spirituality into my dance and teachings. I do so to impassion, empower, and inspire students to deeply understand the meaning of divine love embodied and to explore dance as a powerful means to express emotion, facilitate spiritual healing, and to fully embrace womanhood. Encompassing all of this I offer online community, courses and training, as well as in-person retreats.

End Notes

1. Cicero, *On Divination*, 1.20.
2. We see the Etruscan's in their earliest form as Villanovan's emerging around 1100 BCE in central Italy. The Villanovans are argued to be the earliest established 'culture' of Italy.
3. Emperor Augustus, in his revival of ancient religion created an Etruscan style circular mound mausoleum that was covered in earth and cypress trees. It was completed in 28 BCE and was an impressive imitation, but also a beautiful creation in itself, of the womb shaped Etruscans tombs.
4. Wellard, J., *The Search for the Etruscans*, p.12.
5. 21st April 753 BCE is regarded as the actual Epoch of Rome. However, archaeologists have found evidence of occupation in this area up to around c.1000 BCE.
6. Titus Livy, Roman Historian, known to us as Livy (59 BCE – 17 CE), wrote a History of Rome titled *Ab Urbe Condita* – Written between 27 and 9 BCE, it records the 'The Founding of the City of Rome' from the foundation story through to the reign of the emperor Augustus.
7. The Vestal Virgins, so famous for their temple and eternal flame that was at the centre of Roman life and culture, did in fact pre-date Roman Civilisation. Their flame was alight long before Romulus and Remus.
8. Cicero, *The Nature of the Gods*.
9. Pliny's resource was the earlier Masurius Sabinus, a jurist from the 1st century CE.
10. Mars's woodpecker does figure briefly in a later foundation story of Rome sitting upon the fig tree watching over proceedings. In a pairing that reflects Grecian influence Mars takes on Avian form and works together (even if secondary and detached) with Lupa for the survival of his twins.

11. *De Divinatione* is a philosophical dialogue about Ancient Roman divination written in 44BC by Marcus Tullius Cicero.

12. The Veneti (North East Italy) wolf Goddess Reitia was charged with the protection of the foreigner.

13. Livy, *Ab Urbe Condition* Book 10, Chapter 23.

14. The open-air meeting space of ancient Rome.

15. A famous Augur who pertained events and observed signs.

16. Roller, L., *In Search of God The Mother*.

17. Pliny, *Natural History* Book 15.

18. The Luperci was believed to have been founded by Romulus and Remus themselves and each of the twins was head of a group or collage; the first being Luperci Quinctiales and the second Luperci Fabiani.

19. Ovid, *Fasti*, II, 381 – 474.

20. *Prostitution, Sexuality and Law in Ancient Rome*. Thomas, McGinn.

21. C. G. Jung, *Collected Works*, VOL 9:1, the Archetypes and the Collective Unconscious, para.271.

22. Interestingly sycamore bark can also make a red dye just as the red juice of the fig tree does. Both are symbolic of the sacred blood of the goddess. In reflection of this you can understand why the trees were deemed sacred with their production of both white and red sacred liquids.

23. *Women's Religions in the Greco-Roman World. A Sourcebook*. Edit. By Kraemer, Ross, Shephard, p.37.

24. Ovid, *Fasti*, II, 410. He claimed to complete the writing of his *Fasti* in 8 CE.

25. *"The City of Repair": rituals, gastronomy, and politics at the origins of the modern names for the liver*. Michelle Augusto Riva et al. Hepatol. Nov 2011. National Library of Medicine.

26. Joseph, Campbell, *Oriental Mythology*, p.12.

Bibliography

Primary Sources

Cicero, M., *On Old Age. On Friendship. On Divination.* W.A Falconer (ed. And trans.) (London, Penguin Books, 1989).

Cicero, M., *The Nature of Gods.* P.G Walsh (ed. And trans.) (Oxford, Oxford University Press, 2008).

Livy, T., *The Early History of Rome: Books I-V of the History of Rome from its foundations.* R.M. Ogilvie (trans.) (London, Penguin Classics, 2008).

Ovid., *Fasti.* A Wiseman & P. Wiseman (trans.) (Oxford, Oxford University Press, 2011).

Pliny the Elder., *Natural History.* J. Healey (trans.) (London, Penguin Books, 1991).

Plutarch., *Essays.* R. Waterfield. (trans.) (London, Penguin Books, 1991).

Plutarch., *Fall of the Roman Republic: Six Lives.* R. Seager (trans.) (London, Penguin Books, 2006).

Virgil., *Aeneid.* F. Ahl (trans.) (Oxford, Oxford University Press, 2008).

Secondary Sources

Archer, P. *Rome Alive: A Source Guide to the Ancient City.* (Illinois, Bolchazy-Carducci Publishers, 2004).

Beard, Mary. *SPQR. A History of Ancient Rome.* (London, Profile Books Ltd., 2016).

Campbell, Joseph. *The Masks of God: Occidental Mythology.* (London, Penguin Books, 1992).

Dixon, Suzanne. *The Roman Mother.* (Oxon, Routledge, 2014).

Jung, C. *The Archetypes and the Collective Unconscious.* (London, Routledge, 1968).

Kraemer, Ross, S. *Women's Religions in the Greco-Roman World. A Sourcebook.* (New York, Oxford University Press, 2004).

McGinn, T. *Prostitution, Sexuality and Law in Ancient Rome.* (Oxford, Oxford University Press, 1998).

Roman, M & Roman, Luke. *Aphrodite to Zeus: An encyclopaedia of Greek and Roman Mythology.* (New York, Checkmark Books. 2011).

Holloway, R. *The Archaeology of Early Rome and Latium.* (Abingdon, Routledge, 1996).

Roller, L. E. *In Search of God The Mother. The Cult of Anatolian Cybele.* (London, University of California Press, 1999).

Riva, M. A. (edit) *The City of Repair: rituals, gastronomy, and politics at the origins of the modern names for the liver.* (Digital Paper, National Library of Medicine, Nov 2011).

Simon, E & Thomson De Grummond, N (eds) *The Religion of the Etruscans.* (Austin, University of Texas Press, 2006).

Spivey, N. *Etruscan Art.* (London, Thames and Hudson, 1997).

Staples, A. *From Good Goddess to Vestal Virgins: Sex and Category in Roman Religions.* (London and New York, Routledge, 1998).

Wellard, James. *The Search for the Etruscans.* (Tennessee, Thomas Nelson and Sons Ltd. 1973).

Wildfang, Robin Lorsch. *Rome's Vestal Virgins: A Study of Rome's Vestal Priestesses in the Late Republic and Early Empire.* (Abingdon, Routledge, 2006).

Readers of ebooks can buy or view any of these bestsellers by clicking on the live link in the title. Most titles are published in paperback and as an ebook. Paperbacks are available in traditional bookshops. Both print and ebook formats are available online.

Find more titles and sign up to our readers' newsletter
http://www.johnhuntpublishing.com/paganism

Follow us on Facebook
https://www.facebook.com/MoonBooks

Follow us on Instagram
https://www.instagram.com/moonbooksjhp/

Follow us on Twitter
https://twitter.com/MoonBooksJHP

Follow us on TikTok
https://www.tiktok.com/@moonbooksjhp